THE GUT GIRLS

by Sarah Daniels

SAMUEL FRENCH, INC.
45 WEST 25TH STREET   NEW YORK 10010
7623 SUNSET BOULEVARD HOLLYWOOD 90046
LONDON   TORONTO

IMPORTANT BILLING AND CREDIT REQUIREMENTS

All producers of THE GUT GIRLS *must* give credit to the Author of the Play in all programs distributed in connection with performances of the Play and in all instances in which the title of the Play appears for purposes of advertising, publicizing or otherwise exploiting the Play and/or a production. The name of the Author *must* also appear on a separate line, on which no other name appears, immediately following the title, and *must* appear in size of type not less than fifty percent the size of the title type.

The Gut Girls was first performed at the Albany Empire, London on November 2, 1988. The cast was as follows:

MAGGIE/NORA/EDNA................................ Eve Bland
POLLY .... Joanna Mays
ELLEN/PRISCILLA................................ Cathy Shipton
KATE .... Janet Steel
ANNIE/EMILY/EADY .... Gillian Wright
LADY HELENA..................................... Claire Vousden
HARRY/ARTHUR/LEN/MAD JACKO .... Graham Cull
JIM/EDWIN .... Peter Seton

Directed by Teddy Kiendl
Designed by Kate Owen

The action takes place in Deptford at the turn of the century.

ACT I

Scene 1

The Gutting Shed.

ELLEN, MAGGIE, POLLY and KATE are working. HARRY the foreman, comes in.

HARRY. I've got a new 'un for yer, gils. To replace Maud. (*Calls behind him.*) Come on, petal, they won't eat yer. (*HE shoves ANNIE into the shed.*) That's the least of yer problems. (*HE goes.*)

(ANNIE stares at the sight before her in horror. SHE sways. MAGGIE steps neatly behind her, catching her before she falls.)

MAGGIE. Stand yerself up girl, and whatever you do don't take no deep breaths, that won't do yer no good in here.
ANNIE. I think I'm going to be sick. (*SHE puts her hand over her mouth.*)

(KATE hovers with the mop, in anticipation.)

MAGGIE. (*To Annie.*) Don't think about it. Think about getting paid, think about buying a new hat, being the Queen of England, anything.

KATE. We got enough insides to deal wiv here without clearing up yourn.

ELLEN. (*To Kate.*) Alright little 'un, we've not forgotten how you was on your first day.

KATE. Stop calling me that. Me name's Kate.

ANNIE. (*Holds her nose, gasps.*) It's awful.

POLLY. Nothing wrong with your eyesight, then. That's right. Offal by name, awful by nature. (*Holds up a piece of liver.*) Feeling a bit liverish meself.

(*ANNIE continues to look horrified.*)

MAGGIE. Ain't you never seen meat before?

ANNIE. Not a lot.

KATE. You never seen a butcher's then? C'mon now, we can't stand around all day waiting to ketch yer if yer decides to fall down again.

ELLEN. Give her a chance.

MAGGIE. What's yer name?

ANNIE. Annie.

MAGGIE. I'm Maggie. She's Ellen. Her with the offal jokes is Polly and the little madam here is Kate. You start by helping Kate. Then when we get a chance we'll show you what else you got to do, but you've got to keep your eyes and brain on what you're doing, otherwise you'll end up like Maud.

KATE. (*To Annie.*) Fer now, we just got to keep the floor clean on account of it gets all bloody and it's very bad fer yer health once it gets jellified around yer ankles.

(*JIM, terrified of humiliation, enters staggering under the weight of a heavy carcass.*)

MAGGIE. Having trouble lifting yer meat, Jimbo? Here let me give yer a hand.

KATE. Leave him alone.

(MAGGIE takes the carcass, by contrast handling it with ease, and hangs it up. JIM starts to load pieces of meat into a barrow as fast as he can. The OTHERS carry on as though he wasn't there.)

ELLEN. *(To Maggie.)* What you doing helping him? You know what they're like—give 'em an inch and they tek a yard.

POLLY. More like they think they got a yard when they only got an inch.

(JIM, head down, works even faster.)

MAGGIE. This girl, Maud, used to work here. Best one with the knives she was. Leaves when she gets married. Day after her wedding night, nearly cuts her fingers right off.

ANNIE. How?

POLLY. She was playing cards and she threw her hand in. How d'you think?

ANNIE. But ...

MAGGIE. With the bread knife.

ANNIE. Oh. I thought you said she was thc best one ...

MAGGIE. She was. I'm telling you, right.

ELLEN. Shock of getting married.

MAGGIE. See, all her life she'd been led to believe that something this big *(Indicates two inches.)* was really this big. *(Indicates twelve inches.)* When she finds out on her wedding night—well, severely impaired her judgement.

(JIM goes.)

KATE. I don't know why you always have to start up like that in front of Jim.

POLLY. I feel sorry for him an' all. It's not right at that, that a frail young lad like that should be having to do this sort of work.

ELLEN. Don't forget he's getting paid half again what we are.

MAGGIE. Oh Christ, don't start up on that bleedin' union business.

ANNIE. What happened to her?

POLLY. God told her in a dream: Ellen, you are a leader of women—get them interested in the unions.

ANNIE. No, that woman, Maud.

KATE. They're talking about unions as in trade not as in marriage.

POLLY. She went into production—of offspring.

ANNIE. *(To Ellen.)* You got children, then?

ELLEN. No, I work here.

MAGGIE. No, Maud has. She's like the rest of 'em—a one woman baby show.

ELLEN. What you talking about. She ain't even had her first one yet.

MAGGIE. Give her time.

ELLEN. She don't want no more. I met her down Church Street on Sunday, she said when this one was born she ain't having no more.

POLLY. What's she planning on—becoming a widow?

ELLEN. No, her sister works in the sausage skin factory. That gave her the idea. She tells me if them sausage skins can hold sausages and not split then what's the betting ...

MAGGIE. Not in front of the nipper.

KATE. Who are you calling a nipper? I'm fifteen next birthday and I wouldn't care but you ain't never even got yourself a chap.

MAGGIE. And you've got one so frail that he has trouble carting his own intestines around never mind a hundred weight of cattle tubes.

ANNIE. I still don't understand, what trade are you in, Ellen?

ELLEN. Eh?

POLLY. You mentioned trade unions, remember?

MAGGIE. Polly, did you have to bring that up again?

ELLEN. (*To Annie.*) Oh, right. No, I'm not in one but I'm trying to get one started.

MAGGIE. Leave it out, Ellen, you're worse than a dog with a bone you are. None of us want to go to your boring meetings and read boring books and drink tea with boring people called Jasper, Sebastian and Beatrice.

ELLEN. (*To Annie.*) But I've had a little bit of trouble getting anyone interested.

ANNIE. I only just got here, I don't want to go on strike.

ELLEN. Oh, and do you want to go on working a thirteen hour day in terrible conditions?

MAGGIE. (*To the others.*) Here she goes. Ignore her. Pretend you can't hear.

ELLEN. Being treated like you're not worth a light. No pay when you're ill. No compensation when you chop your hand off. Laid off with no warning.

(HARRY comes in.)

HARRY. I'm sure Mr. Cuttle-Smythe would be very interested to hear your views.

ELLEN. Oh, blimey, I never heard you come in.

HARRY. 'Course you never.

MAGGIE. She was only joking, Harry.

HARRY. Mister Dedham to you. None of you are indispensable—right, not one, so just remember that. *(To Annie.)* Don't let them corrupt you dear, they're scum this lot, each and every one of them. How come a little flower like yerself couldn't do better than this?

ANNIE. I don't know Mister Dedham.

(HE tweaks Annie's ear.)

POLLY. *(Winks at Kate.)* Oh, Harry, some fat's got stuck in the bloody gully, quick.

HARRY. Let's have a look then.

POLLY. *(Picks up the fat.)* Oh. I've got it. *(Offering it to Harry.)* You going outside?

HARRY. *(Takes it.)* Oh, give it here.

POLLY. Ta.

(HARRY goes.)

KATE. *(To Annie.)* You gotta watch him. Always hold the mop like this. Wiv the handle sticking out at the end.

If he comes up behind you, pretend you don't know and then just jab the broom right back inter his turkey gristle.

ANNIE. Do you get turkeys here then?

MAGGIE. Yeah, 'cept they're still walking around on two legs, giving orders.

KATE. (*To Annie.*) 'Ere, how old are you?

ANNIE. Sixteen.

KATE. Oh. Aye. Where you bin?

ANNIE. Nowhere.

(*Pause.*)

MAGGIE. Where d'you live now?

ANNIE. St. John's.

ELLEN. Oh? St. John's, eh? You still live with your mum and dad? (*ANNIE shakes her head.*) What you got, a room then? (*ANNIE doesn't respond.*)

MAGGIE. Leave it Ellen.

ELLEN. Well, where … Oh, you in that house, ain't yer, fer friendless girls.

(*ANNIE nods but hangs her head in shame.*
Pause.)

MAGGIE. So you had a baby then?

ANNIE. Born dead.

ELLEN. What you looking at the floor for? We ain't judging you.

ANNIE. Everybody else does.

POLLY. Expect they do while you got that address.

MAGGIE. You'd be better off getting yerself a decent place to live.

ELLEN. There's a room going, in the house where I am, if you want, you can come and see it this evening.

ANNIE. They say I got to stay where I am.

MAGGIE. What fer?

ANNIE. Prevention. Stop me being loose living. That's why I couldn't go back into service an' had to work here.

(Silence. Annie has offended them.)

POLLY. Ellen was in service, weren't yer Ellen? Gave it up specially so as she could work here.

ANNIE. What happened to you then?

ELLEN. It suited neither my health nor my temperament. In fact I only lasted a day.

ANNIE. Lord Jesus, you must have done something terrible.

ELLEN. They done something terrible to me. I was thirteen right, and the boy was a year younger than me. His mother was in the room, mind, she didn't turn a hair. He threw his shoes at me and said, "clean these at once." I said "Excuse me, poppet, but may I suggest you shove 'em up your arse hole."

ANNIE. You was lucky you had somewhere else to go.

MAGGIE. *(To Annie.)* I tell you girl, you may think this place is hell but we get paid in one week nearly what you get for a whole year in service, so by comparison it makes this place seem more like paradise.

POLLY. Except the only difference is, you didn't have to wear no clothes in the Garden of Eden. If you don't wear two coats in this cold hole you'll be in a wooden overcoat before you can say foot and mouth.

(JIM tries to enter without them seeing him. THEY pretend they haven't, although THEY start a conversation for his "benefit." ANNIE looks worried, frightened that they may say something about her past in front of Jim.)

ELLEN. Now this place in St. John's, didn't I read in the Kentish Mercury, I think it was, that they was pulling it down and going to put in its place a building so enormous it could fit the whole cattle market into it.

MAGGIE. *(Looks at her.)* Did yer?

(ELLEN winks at Maggie.)

POLLY. Oh yeah. Now you come to say it, I remember that an' all.

ELLEN. It's going to be changed into a refuge for loose and fallen men.

KATE. Pull the other one.

POLLY. That's right. Any man who's so much as showed himself to anyone other than the midwife who delivered him is going to have to live there.

(JIM glances at Kate. KATE is looking at Polly, but MAGGIE sees Jim.)

MAGGIE. *(To Kate.)* And even ones who look at women will have to go there, for prevention is better than cure. *(ELLEN joins in.)*

KATE. Huh, that'll be the day.

(THEY laugh. JIM scurries out.)

ANNIE. Please, please don't say nothing about me in front of the men.

ELLEN. Don't worry. We know what it's like if they find out, they think you're fair game.

KATE. What you on about? Most blokes out there think we're rubbish. I mean as far as they're concerned, there's only one thing worse than being a gut girl and that's being a whore.

ELLEN. Time for tea. Kate tek Annie with yer so as you can show 'er.

KATE. (*Looks round to make sure they're not overheard.*) You don't want to mind their talk. They're all right.

ANNIE. Polly seems nice. The other two frighten me. Seem real hard.

KATE. Listen, right, 'cos I thought that. I still do, especially about that Ellen. Then last Christmas me mother died. I was right upset. She made us promise she wouldn't have no pauper's burial. I tried to reason with her. I says, you never would've spent that much money on yerself when you was alive, why worry when you ain't even going to be there to see it.

ANNIE. I know but the old 'uns are funny that way aren't they?

KATE. We done everything, but we never had enough money. It was Ellen, what stood outside the gate here on payday 'til she'd collected enough. And she jus' give it to me. Not a word, nothing. C'mon they'll all be moanin' an' groaning fer their tea. Don't worry you'll be all right.

(THEY go. Crossfade to MAGGIE, POLLY and ELLEN.)

MAGGIE. Where have they got to?

ELLEN. Wherever it is, if they don't get back here soon they'll have me to answer to, never mind Harry.

MAGGIE. Oh, hark at you.

POLLY. *(Sings.)* The working class can kiss my arse. I've got the foreman's job at last.

ELLEN. Oh, yes. How can a woman become a foreman?

MAGGIE. Can't you talk about anything other than rights and wrongs and this way, that way, state of how things should be nonsense.

(KATE and ANNIE return carrying the cans of tea.)

POLLY. *(Looking at the tea.)* Bloody hell. It isn't weak, it's helpless.

MAGGIE. *(Taking a mouthful.)* And it's cold.

KATE. *(Excited.)* Forget the tea. Forget the tea. Guess who we just saw—only Lady Helena and Lord Tartaden.

POLLY. What was they doing—walking on the water?

KATE. No, they're here. In the market.

MAGGIE. Butcher's shut—and she's run out of devilled kidneys.

KATE. No, no, she's come to look at us all working.

POLLY. What does she think we are, a side show?

ELLEN. It'll be about that club she set up—a non-starter if ever I heard one.

ANNIE. What club?

MAGGIE. We don't rightly know. Some do-goody thing run by some interfering ladies with Jesus between the ears. We're supposed to go down there but we don't really fancy it.

POLLY. By all accounts, she's never shown her face in there and I bet my life she won't bother to poke her nose in here either.

(LADY HELENA and LORD EDWIN TARTADEN appear at the other end of the shed. HARRY seems intent on preventing them from entering.)

HARRY. Oh no, me lady. I implore you. You don't want to come in here. It's not fer someone of your sensibilities.

LADY HELENA. My good man. I am the best judge of my sensibilities. The very purpose of my visit is to meet these young ladies.

HARRY. Ladies? Oh your highness, how you compliment them. Why their language would knock you sideways—it's enough to stagger a horse.

LADY HELENA. I think you are forgetting that I experienced my poor husband bleed to death. His language was choice, forgivable in the circumstances, but choice.

EDWIN. *(To Harry.)* I shall see that no harm befalls the Duchess. So be a good chap and allow us through.

HARRY. *(Nervously.)* Well, of course.

(LADY HELENA and EDWIN advance. HARRY goes. POLLY, MAGGIE and ELLEN work with vigour and perhaps a little unnecessary vulgarity. ANNIE gazes, stunned by admiration. KATE too, is a little in awe. SHE mops the floor frantically trying to make it a more

acceptable place for Lady Helena's feet. EDWIN takes one look.)

EDWIN. Oh my. *(Softly.)* Oh my. *(Faintly.)* Oh my.

(HE collapses on the floor. MAGGIE is near enough to him to have caught him but SHE continues with her work.)

LADY HELENA. Oh dear, dearie me. *(Calls.)* Foreman. Would it be possible to give Lord Tartaden a cup of tea?

(HARRY rushes in, puts his hands under Edwin's armpits and drags him off.)

LADY HELENA. I really must apologise for Lord Tartaden. Oh please carry on with your work.

ANNIE. *(Blurts out.)* That nearly happened to me this morning. It's my first day like 'so I know what it feels like.

LADY HELENA. I suppose in time one becomes accustomed to it. I don't suppose you ever find it pleasant though. What's your name?

ANNIE. Annie. And—er—this is Ellen, Polly, Kate and Maggie.

LADY HELENA. Pleased to meet you. How many young women are there working in this market?

(Silence.)

ELLEN. Well, there's about fifty in each shed and there's ten sheds in all, so it's above five hundred.

LADY HELENA. And what sort of work, I mean, what does your job entail?

POLLY. Put your finger right on it, madam, entrails.

MAGGIE. Chop up animal flesh, sorting and cleaning the tubes from the hearts, livers, kidneys, lungs and that.

ELLEN. Getting the meat ready for how you find it in the butcher's basically.

LADY HELENA. Hence the collective noun for you all: The Gut Girls *(THEY look at her.)* Oh I'm quite *au fait* with the word "gut"—and I often have to use the word belly—in the context of asking my cook occasionally if we may have *(Whispers.)* belly of pork.

POLLY. Oh right. *(Wraps up a piece of pork.)* There you go. *(Gives it to Lady Helena.)* Don't say nothing.

LADY HELENA. Thank you very much, but no, *(Giving the meat back.)* I don't think so. The purpose of my visit was to talk to you.

MAGGIE. Oh?

LADY HELENA. Are all the women working here as young as you?

KATE. Mostly, 'cos of course they leave when they gets married and that, but there a few old 'uns like nearly thirty.

LADY HELENA. And do you become rather demoralised working here?

POLLY. We got as much morals as the next person, lady.

ELLEN. Yes we do. The conditions we work in, as you can see, leave a lot of room for improvement.

MAGGIE. Shut it, Ellen. Lady Helena don't want to know about that.

LADY HELENA. But I do. I have heard about this place. And I wanted to see it for myself. I agree with you, it is gruesome work.

ANNIE. Someone's got to do it, I suppose.

LADY HELENA. I don't know if you know but I have set up a club for you, for any young women working here—in Creek Road, not two minutes walk away.

MAGGIE. We did hear about it.

LADY HELENA. I am baffled as to why it's been so poorly attended.

POLLY. To be honest with you, we don't have the time.

ELLEN. Life's too short.

MAGGIE. Life's for the livers.

LADY HELENA. But it's in the evening. It doesn't start until seven.

POLLY. But we don't knock off 'til eight.

LADY HELENA. So then what do you do?

MAGGIE. Most of us have to go home, help get the tea, put our younger brothers and sisters to bed.

ELLEN. Sleep. We have to be back here at seven in the morning.

LADY HELENA. Don't you have any time for yourselves at all?

POLLY. We might have a drink after work, go to the music hall occasionally.

LADY HELENA. But the club, the whole purpose of it, is for you. To give you some time for yourselves, something specially for you. Not work, whether it's here or at home but a place to go that's warm and safe and great fun.

(THEY all look rather unsure.)

LADY HELENA. There's a piano, we have coffee and cake. And plenty of other things.

MAGGIE. What d'you want ter go wasting yer time with us fer? We got jobs and homes. There's them far worse off than us. You've no need to bother yerself we're all right as we is, honest.

LADY HELENA. Your unselfish attitude is commendable but I have done other things in this area, for other people and I thought it was time that you, the young ladies of Deptford got a piece of the cake. Your well-being is now, well, my concern.

POLLY. No need to concern yerself further, now you've seen us. *(Holds up her arm to display her biceps.)* See, we're strong as oxes.

LADY HELENA. Please say you'll think about it.

MAGGIE. We'll do that all right.

ELLEN. *(Mutters.)* That's about all we'll do.

KATE. Oh, we will, madam.

LADY HELENA. Well, next port of call, the sheep-gutting sheds.

POLLY. No, they ain't got no morals, what they got is offal.

LADY HELENA. Pardon?

POLLY. Offal.

LADY HELENA. Sorry?

POLLY. Entails only entrails. Just a joke like.

LADY HELENA. I'll say goodbye for now but I do hope you give the club a try. You won't regret it. It was nice to talk with you. *(SHE shakes hands with them all.)* Polly, Kate, Annie, Maggie, Ellen.

(THEY all look aghast as her white glove becomes blood stained but SHE appears not to notice. SHE goes.)

ANNIE. *(Looks at her hand in wonderment.)* I don't think I'll ever wash it again.

ELLEN. If you carries on looking at it like that, boggled-eyed, and you starts chopping, you won't have to wash it, you'll hack it off.

KATE. She was lovely though weren't she? See that dress on her—what it must've cost.

ELLEN. Hark at yer. I thought you didn't like toffs.

KATE. She ain't no toff. She's related to royalty. Yer saw how she was with us, spoke to us like we was taking tea with her or something.

ANNIE. She might be dressed expensive but didn't she look comical.

POLLY. Yeah, she never even had no earrings—poor cow.

ELLEN. If you ask me, she wants us out of here, so men can have our jobs.

KATE. Don't talk stupid—they wouldn't do this job. It's only a club she's set up.

(HARRY comes in.)

HARRY. Fancy her stooping to visit you lot. I bet you showed us up good and proper.

ELLEN. She were asking after you Harry, weren't she gils?

HARRY. You. How many times do I have ter tell you. You call me Mister Dedham. (*Then.*) What d'you mean, asking after me?

MAGGIE. She says ter us, she says, with a little like shiver in her voice, who's that handsome bulky foreman?

HARRY. Go on wiv yer.

ELLEN. She reckons to us that she'd really like to let her hair down with a body like yourn.

HARRY. That's quite enough. (*But preening himself.*)

MAGGIE. So you'd better watch out Mister Dedham 'cos it's been two years since her husband bled to death. Maybe she wants to see it 'appen again.

HARRY. Now you've all stopped to have a good boggle at a lady, something you lot will never be if yer lives to be a hundred, don't think you'll be stopping again for yer dinner break. Also we don't want yer sloping off outside 'cos they're unloading. We don't want the cows getting frightened before they reach the slaughtering pens. (*HE goes.*)

ELLEN. But Harry, we need some fresh air.

HARRY. (*Comes back.*) Well, if yer go out there the air wouldn't be fresh no more. You lot would turn it rancid.

MAGGIE. (*Bringing her knife down.*) Time we done something about him.

ELLEN. Well, what have I been on about these weeks, eh? Organising ourselves.

POLLY. Right girls, it's pork sandwiches tomorrow.

MAGGIE. Say no more.

ANNIE. Do they, like, give us a discount then?

POLLY. Very generous discount. Don't you worry.

ELLEN. I don't know how you can possibly eat the stuff when yer see what happens to it all day.

POLLY. Except Ellen, who'll be sticking to her lettuce sandwiches through thick and thin.

MAGGIE. She only eats rabbit food, 'er. If she's not careful she'll end up with rickets.

ELLEN. You don't know what you're talking about, you don't.

POLLY. (*To Annie.*) It's these modern people she's acquainted with.

MAGGIE. She'll be riding one of them bicycles next, you wait.

ELLEN. Leave it out.

ANNIE. What modern people?

POLLY. Troublemakers.

MAGGIE. This little band of educated pilgrims what go round stirring up folks. First she fell in with the fish filleting lot, then with the fur pullers. She tries to do fer workers what John Wesley done fer Methodists.

ANNIE. What's that got to do with eating lettuce?

POLLY. Oh my dear, they wouldn't be seen dead eating flesh.

ANNIE. (*Gags.*) I don't feel ...

ELLEN. Go outside.

ANNIE. But he ... oh, hell! I'll have ter ... (*SHE goes.*)

ELLEN. I suppose I'd better go and see ...

MAGGIE. Leave it. You heard what Harry said.

KATE. She won't want us standing over her anyway.

POLLY. I thought she'd got used to it. I never meant to ... well.

MAGGIE. It weren't you mentioning meat what done it. It was you mentioning bleeding lettuce.

ELLEN. Some of us will never get used to it. Don't you think it's cruel, what happens to those defenceless animals?

POLLY. At least they got the chance to run away. You should spare a thought for them poor lettuces, Ellen, just sitting there waiting for you to rip 'em up, without hope of escape.

KATE. We're bleeding lucky we get to eat meat. Before I worked here, if we saw any at home, it would go to me dad and me brothers.

MAGGIE. And, Ellen, if no bugger ate meat, we wouldn't have no jobs would we?

Scene 2

Lady Helena's drawing room. SHE has changed her clothes. The clothes she wore to the Foreign Cattle Market are in a pile on the floor.

LADY HELENA. Enter.
EMILY. Lord Tartaden is here to see you, madam.

(The clothes stink to high heaven and EMILY tries not to sniff obviously, but at the same time tries to work out what the smell is.)

LADY HELENA. Thank you, Emily. Show him in, please.

EMILY. Very good, madam. (*SHE goes.*)

LADY HELENA. (*Calls.*) Oh Emily ...

EMILY. (*Comes back.*) Yes, madam?

LADY HELENA. Would you please take these clothes to Johnson and instruct him to burn them.

EMILY. (*Looking at the pile.*) As you say madam. (*SHE bends to pick them up but then looks up.*) Begging your pardon, but all of them, madam?

LADY HELENA. Yes, yes. (*Then.*) Oh I see that you mean. Yes, there are one or two delicate items of undergarment there. (*These should be the most enormous, heavy-boned corsets imaginable.*) Not an altogether savoury task for a man. No not at all. Would you perhaps take it upon yourself to dispose of them for me?

EMILY. Yes, madam. (*SHE picks up the pile of clothes, staggers to the door, the smell nearly knocking her over.*)

LADY HELENA. Oh Emily.

EMILY. (*Turns.*) Yes, madam?

LADY HELENA. They, the others, call you Emy— don't they?

EMILY. (*Unnerved.*) Why, yes, madam.

LADY HELENA. Could you spare a couple of moments of your time. Take a seat. Emy. I like that. It sounds friendly.

(*Surprised, EMILY does so. Still carrying the clothes throughout the conversation it appears that LADY HELENA can't smell anything, while EMILY tries not show that she is reeling from the stench.*)

LADY HELENA. I've had a rather interesting morning, Emy. I've been on a jaunt around Deptford.

EMILY. (*Aghast.*) Deptford?

LADY HELENA. Umm. Do you come from there?

EMILY. Why no, M'lady, I come from (*Proudly.*) Hatcham Park.

LADY HELENA. Well, I have set up a club for the young ladies working in the Foreign Cattle market and this morning I paid them a visit.

EMILY. (*Blurts out.*) The Gut Girls? Begging your pardon, madam, I don't know what you want to go bothering with them for.

LADY HELENA. That is it, isn't it? The world knows what they do for a living and has labelled them accordingly. By themselves they are hardly likely to find the incentive to fight against becoming rough and unladylike.

EMILY. Well, come to think of it, no other employer would want to touch them with a barge pole.

LADY HELENA. What I cannot understand is why they are so reluctant to attend the club. They gave me one reason, and I'm seeing Mr. Cuttle-Smythe this afternoon about that, but I wondered if you had any suggestions.

EMILY. I would think that if you were there in person, as it were, it would make a world of difference.

LADY HELENA. But the ladies who run it are so much better at it than me.

EMILY. But they're not you.

LADY HELENA. Umm. No, you're quite right, they're not. Thank you Emily.

EMILY. What for, madam?

LADY HELENA. An excellent idea. I'm not going to give up on this. Every time I think of those poor creatures my heart goes out to them.

EMILY. Poor is one thing they're not. Not really, madam.

LADY HELENA. Oh my goodness, I'd forgotten all about Lord Tartaden. Please tell him to come straight through.

(EMILY goes. EDWIN TARTADEN comes in. HE kisses Helena's hand by way of greeting.)

EDWIN. Helena ... *(HE kneels.)*

LADY HELENA. Oh Tarty, please stop making a fool of yourself.

EDWIN. If I were a brave man I would ask for your hand.

LADY HELENA. Get up this instant, stop being so ridiculous.

EDWIN. You are peeved at my untimely departure from the cattle market. My manhood has let you down.

LADY HELENA. Your manhood is neither here nor there to me. I have asked you here to enlist your support. As a friend. That's all.

EDWIN. I will do anything to win your affection.

LADY HELENA. Time to drop this toddle talk Tarty. To business. Now you didn't meet those poor children this morning.

EDWIN. No, how impolite of me, I forgot to ask, how did it go?

LADY HELENA. I met a good number. Their talk was, well, strangely ill-mannered.

EDWIN. In what way?

LADY HELENA. Well, they spoke to me as if I was any old body.

EDWIN. Oh how dreadful, Helena.

LADY HELENA. It wasn't really. Actually, it was rather refreshing.

EDWIN. (*Squashed.*) Oh.

LADY HELENA. It was a revelation. Really, I don't know what I'd expected. I suppose, a rather mind-numbed, dreary collection of girls, but they were full of vigour, actually laughed and chatted with me. I think, well I hope, that they were as intrigued with me as I was with them. But those sheds, the airlessness, the smell.

EDWIN. Don't remind me.

LADY HELENA. Covered in stomach linings. Some of them working up to their ankles in blood.

EDWIN. Please, Helena, spare me.

LADY HELENA. How would you like to sort through livers, lungs, hearts, kidneys.

EDWIN. Offal.

LADY HELENA. Yes, it is. Awful. (*Pause, then giggles.*) Oh, that was it, the joke about being offal, I see now.

EDWIN. Sorry?

LADY HELENA. Just something they said. Imagine, Edwin, being pushed into those working conditions at a tender age. No wonder they appear so rough. They have to be. It's disgraceful. I cannot believe what we're breeding.

EDWIN. Or not breeding. The fact of the matter is that there is a grave concern for the high infant mortality rate among the lower echelons *vis-a-vis* will there be enough healthy young men for the Army in the next generation?

LADY HELENA. And where does the fault lie?

EDWIN. With the women, who else? They go out to work like men, drink like men, curse, well—you met them. Some even have started to deny, and here you must excuse my unpardonable frankness, deny their menfolk marital relations for fear of ...

LADY HELENA. I should imagine, when one has very little money, feeding one's children and oneself becomes an arduous task.

EDWIN. Lack of money may indeed affect the mortality rate but it is a poor excuse for having no ...

LADY HELENA. I'm not concerned about their relations, but about them *vis-a-vis* their squalid existence.

(EMILY enters.)

EMILY. Mr. Cuttle-Smythe to see you, madam.

LADY HELENA. Please show him in.

(EMILY goes.)

EDWIN. If it makes you happy you shall have my support.

LADY HELENA. Thank you.

(EMILY enters with Mr. Cuttle-Smythe.)

LADY HELENA. Mr. Cuttle-Smythe, how lovely to see you. It's so kind of you to call by at such short notice.

ARTHUR. Not at all. The pleasure is all mine, Lady Helena, Lord Tartaden.

LADY HELENA. I'll come straight to the point Mr. Cuttle-Smythe. I've asked you here because my information tells me that you own a large proportion of the Foreign Cattle Market.

ARTHUR. You elevate my status too highly. I wish I did, alas, I am merely a partner of a firm which owns some of the gutting sheds.

LADY HELENA. Ah, that's what I'm interested in.

ARTHUR. Really? You'd like to make me an offer?

LADY HELENA. Pardon?

ARTHUR. I thought, sorry. That you were interested in buying …

LADY HELENA. I am sorry to disappoint you, but what I actually wanted to ask you for was a favour.

ARTHUR. Oh, well, by all means. If I can be of help—

LADY HELENA. I would like you to give the girls permission to leave work an hour earlier on a Thursday evening as an incentive for them to attend my girl's club.

ARTHUR. But that's a lot of working hours, Mam. With due respect. Do you realise what you are asking for?

LADY HELENA. I'm sure you could use your influence.

ARTHUR. And, I was going to say, that it's not really up to me. (*Pause.*) Of course, I will ask.

LADY HELENA. Thank you. And your wife, how is she? I was rather hoping she might accompany you this afternoon.

ARTHUR. She—er—I'm afraid she—er—had another commitment.

LADY HELENA. I did meet her at Lady Somerville's. We were given a talk about the life and work of Dr.

Garrison, the Argentine missionary extraordinaire—a thoroughly inspiring evening it was too.

ARTHUR. Oh,yes?

LADY HELENA. It occurred to me that your wife, Priscilla, if I remember correctly, might like to help me with my work in Deptford?

ARTHUR. Well, you see, how can I put it, my wife is rather withdrawn, not a person who is readily at ease in social situations. I don't mean to undermine her, but I don't think she'd be suited to that sort of thing. To be brutally frank, she suffers from melancholy.

LADY HELENA. Please just ask her to call on me. After all, it's not really a social situation we're talking about.

ARTHUR. Certainly, I will, Lady Helena. (*Shakes her hand.*) Lord Tartaden.

(*ARTHUR goes.*)

EDWIN. Even our Lord only turned water into wine not—

LADY HELENA. I was born to privilege and I am aware of it. Please don't hold a candle for me, Tarty. I will never marry again. I am going to dedicate the rest of my life to charitable work.

EDWIN. You will forgo your own happiness for the sake of the lowest of the low. Oh yes, Helena, even by their own kind they are seen as marginally better than whores.

LADY HELENA. Edwin Tartaden, may I remind you that you are speaking to me.

EDWIN. It is my broken heart talking.

LADY HELENA. Well curb it. And, if you want my opinion it is the men who live off those unfortunate women who are the lowest of the low.

EDWIN. You are so exquisite when you're serious.

LADY HELENA. And so would you be. If you really knew of the plight of these poor, wretched, miserable girls.

Scene 3

Those poor miserable GIRLS, wearing wonderful hats and earrings are laughing and giggling on their way out of work. MAGGIE and ELLEN support ANNIE who appears to be unable to walk unaided.

HARRY. Oi!

ELLEN. Hold up. Keep still. Harry's here.

(THEY stop, terrified. ALL look serious. ANNIE looks terrified.)

POLLY. (*To Annie.*) Look down at the floor, gil, it shows on yer boat.

HARRY. What's going on here? Oi, what's the matter with her?

ELLEN. Are you a doctor now then, Mr. Dedham?

HARRY. Oh no. What's happened? We renounce all liability.

MAGGIE. Well, in this case, rest easy, 'cos it ain't under no circumstances your responsibility.

HARRY. What is?

MAGGIE. You ought to be ashamed of yerself, grown man not bein' able to guess. *(Whispers.)* Women's troubles.

HARRY. *(Embarrassed.)* Oh. *(Disgusted.)* Well, don't just stand there, shift yourselves.

(HE goes. THEY continue walking.)

POLLY. Come on Annie, we only got ter get as far as the Brown Bear.

ANNIE. Can't we just go to that one—The Seaman's Arms?

POLLY. You're joking.

KATE. Come on gel, best foot forward.

MAN. *(Off, shouts.)* You're quiet tonight gels!

MAGGIE. Sing! Sing something.

(ANNIE starts singing, quite seriously, "Jesus bids us shine, with a pure, clear light." The OTHERS stop, horrified.)

MAGGIE. Bloody hell! No, not that, Jesus Christ. *(SHE starts singing "Joshua, Joshua ..." The OTHERS join in.)*

BERT. *(Voice off.)* Oh Gawd, Charlie, the gut girls is out.

CHARLIE. *(Voice off.)* Quick, duck down Queen Street.

MAGGIE. *(Calls after them.)* You goin' to stand us all a drink then, mate?

(The WOMEN laugh.)

ELLEN. (*Calls.*) Where are you off to in such a hurry? Come back here.

(*THEY go into the Brown Bear. LEN the Publican, is less than welcoming. HE is also rather intimidated by them.*)

LEN. Now look girls, how many more ...

MAGGIE. (*Interrupting him. Leans across at him menacingly.*) We ain't girls, right Len? We're ladies, got it?

LEN. Oh yeah, since when?

ELLEN. Since today. When the Duchess of Deptford took lunch with us.

LEN. Oh yeah. (*About their bloodstained coats.*) Spilt her best claret down yer did she?

MAGGIE. Less lip and more service is called for Len.

LEN. Listen girls, ladies. Whatever. You've got your own places to have a drink in. Since you bin coming in here, chaps don't feel safe. It's killing off me custom.

KATE. We're better custom than the blokes. Where's our beers?

LEN. Ladies drink gin.

ELLEN. Ah, now that's the thing about being a lady, you have the choice and you know what ours is.

ANNIE. My leg, my leg, I think it's broken.

MAGGIE. Now look what you made us forget. Don't look, have a bit of decency, turn yer back.

(*LEN turns obediently and gets the drinks. KATE and POLLY bend down and untie the piece of meat strapped to Annie's leg.*)

ANNIE. It's numb. I can't feel it.

POLLY. Give it a rub.

ELLEN. (*To Len.*) What you gawping at? Mek yerself useful and bolt the door.

MAGGIE. (*To Annie.*) Is that better?

ANNIE. (*Nods.*) Ouch. Pins and needles.

POLLY. It'll go off. (*SHE lifts the piece of meat.*)

ELLEN. Newspaper, Len.

LEN. Oh, mind me tables, girls.

POLLY. (*Drops the meat. None too delicately onto a stool which then collapses under the weight.*) Oops.

LEN. Watch it. Watch it. The furniture doesn't grow on trees. Bleedin' hell.

ELLEN. Stop bellyaching Len. Them things are riddled. Wonder the woodworm ain't soiled the meat.

(*POLLY lifts the meat to the next table more gently. MAGGIE takes her knife and swiftly chops it into pieces.*)

MAGGIE. Stinking joint.

ELLEN. I'm pleased you're coming round to my point of view. (*SHE wraps the meat.*)

KATE. What you grumbling 'bout. This was fresh in today.

MAGGIE. I weren't meaning the meat, I was talking about Len's piss pot of a pub.

POLLY. Well, we ain't stopping in here much longer, are we.

(*LEN brings them their pints.*)

MAGGIE. You can unlock the door now, Len.
LEN. No point, nobody's going to come in while you lot are still in here.

(*ELLEN and MAGGIE lift ANNIE onto the table.*)

POLLY. Here's to your first day, Annie.

(*THEY all raise their glasses. ANNIE takes a delicate sip. The REST OF THEM down it in one.*)

LEN. (*Sees Annie.*) Bleedin' hell.
ANNIE. Let's go down that club on Thursday.
ELLEN. You'd be better off coming to the Union Meeting, you would.
MAGGIE. (*To Ellen.*) You know why you don't like ol' Lady Helena—'cos you're a bit the same. She's trying to get us in one club and you're trying to get us in another.
POLLY. An' if Harry had his way, we'd all be in the club.

(*Awkward silence. ANNIE cringes.*)

ELLEN. Come on Annie, me and you going to find you a new place to live.
ANNIE. I told yer—they won't let me leave.
ELLEN. We'll see about that.

POLLY. I better get off home meself.
KATE. C'mon then.

(THEY finish their drinks and stand.)

LEN. 'Ere, where you off to?
POLLY. Somewhere where the stools ain't shit, and
can stand up by themselves.
MAGGIE. You want a couple of bottles to tek away,
Polly?
POLLY. Yeah, ta.
MAGGIE. And four to tek out, Len.

*(POLLY picks up the broken table and puts it under her
    arm.)*

LEN. *(With four bottles in his hand.)* What you doing,
you can't mek off with that.
POLLY. Getting out of your way, Len. It's only
littering up your establishment, lowering the tone.
LEN. That's a shilling you owe me all told.
MAGGIE. Behave yourself you mutton head. *(SHE
puts a packet of meat on the bar.)* Since when did we
shortchange you?

(POLLY, ELLEN, ANNIE and KATE go.)

LEN. 'Ere Maggie, you ain't looking fer a husband yet
are yer?
MAGGIE. I ain't likely ter find one if I stop in here
jawing with you, am I? What anyone would be wanting
one for beats me.

LEN. Oh.

MAGGIE. What's it to you anyway?

LEN. Ter tell the truth, we get some rough fellas in here and that. I don't mind admitting it, they fair put the wind up me, but with you here like beside me, I don't think I'd ever feel frightened again.

MAGGIE. Oh Len, you're such a lump of lard. (*SHE ruffles his hair, accidentally nearly knocking his head off and goes.*)

LEN. (*With admiration.*) What a woman.

(*LADY HELENA, who has been sitting in her corner, reading the Bible throughout this, now closes it and her eyes.*)

LADY HELENA. Dear Father, who knowest all things, please hear your servant at this time. Give me the strength and comfort which helped to sustain me through my husband's illness. That I, who know the despair and ugliness which suffering brings, might use my knowledge to thy purpose. Please, I ask that you might grant me the grace to overcome my awkwardness with these girls and give me the humanity to remember that we are all your children, equal in your eyes. Guide me along the path thou has chosen for me. That I might share the gifts which in thy graciousness thou hast bestowed upon me. In the hope that through me they will learn of thy everlasting love. Amen.

Scene 4

Polly's mum (EDNA) sits in a chair, peeling potatoes,
although she doesn't let it show, she is really pleased to
see her daughter. POLLY comes in, two bottles of stout
in one hand, the broken table in the other and the meat
under her arm.

POLLY. Oi! Mother!

EDNA. Taken up totting, 'ave we? (*Meaning the table.*)

POLLY. Jus' fell apart in me hands down Len's.

EDNA. How come you got to take it home?

POLLY. Public bar ain't it? Public's entitled to it.
Thought them next door be glad of it fer firewood.

EDNA. They chopped up the shutters today. Ain't got
one stick of furniture in there now. I offers him that chair
we got upstairs, says look it's no use to me, I can't get up
there but he wouldn't hear of it. Pride, pride, pride. It's a
good thing God knows, but it'll carry 'em all off ter the
workshouse.

POLLY. I'll chuck it over their yard right. Then you go
out an' do one of your carry ons about this street bein' used
for tipping rubbish, and that way he'll think by burning it
he'll be doing us a favour.

EDNA. I said to him, I said, what you going to do
when the vicar comes round and he ain't got nothing but
bare floorboards to rest his arse on.

POLLY. I'm sure if Jesus stooped to a stable, the vicar
can manage. 'Ere now talking of stooping guess who came
round and spoke to us all today—Our Lady of Deptford.

EDNA. What fer?

POLLY. I dunno. So as she could have a butchers I s'pose.

EDNA. She didn't want no quarter of tripe. It smells.

POLLY. Thank Gawd you reminded me. (*SHE takes the meat from under her arm and put's it in Edna's lap.*)

EDNA. Well, that'll have plenty of flavour that will, feels half cooked already.

POLLY. I'll go and start it shall I?

EDNA. In a minute, sit down and tell us about your day.

POLLY. Where's the boys?

EDNA. Misbehaved at school today, so I sent 'em to bed without no supper.

POLLY. Oh, you never.

EDNA. Don't worry, I weakened about half an hour ago—took 'em up some bread and a scrape. So, have you got any more gossip?

POLLY. New girl started—Annie—ter take Maud's place. Fallen woman like.

EDNA. Public bars, fallen women, appearances from the gentry. You sure you been to work and not to the music hall.

POLLY. What do you mean it "smells"?

EDNA. Them types poking their noses in. Oh, yes, with the best intentions granted, but mark my words, they always end up making things worse.

POLLY. I don't see how they can though. I mean as long as people eat meat, I'll always have a job. The only thing that could make anything worse is the barmy idea that you've only got to eat vegetables.

EDNA. Well, don't waste no time worrying over that—it'll never catch on. Talking of daft ideas, how is Ellen the mouth?

(Fade to ANNIE and ELLEN.)

Scene 5

ELLEN. This is my room.

ANNIE. Blimey, it's so tidy.

ELLEN. When I moved in I, well, I wanted it to look different than me home. Everything there was so cluttered.

ANNIE. And all them books. Was them shelves here?

ELLEN. No, I made them. I'll show you how if you want some in your room.

ANNIE. I can hardly believe it. You didn't half stand up to her—Mrs. Pickles at the home.

ELLEN. *(Mimicking Mrs. Pickles.)* Are you sure, Annie dear child? Deptford is such a grotesquely insalubrious area with all manner of temptations to corrode a young woman's moral conduct.

ANNIE. I know she was a silly bat and that, but she can't help the way she talks and she done all right by me.

ELLEN. What? Shut up in a prison with the Holy Trinity for breakfast, dinner and tea and a load of hoity-toity nonsense in between.

ANNIE. I never 'ad no place else to go did I? It was them, or the streets, or the workhouse. Yeah, so I got the lectures, the looking down the nose, but I tell you one thing, it's a lot easier to stomach when you ain't starving hungry. I was fed proper there, they saw to that.

ELLEN. What about yer chap then? Buggered off I suppose. (*Pause.*) Would you like me to help paint your room?

ANNIE. No, no it's all right. I like that paper. (*Suddenly.*) He weren't my chap were he? And he's not buggered off nowhere. He's still living the life of Riley fer all I knows.

ELLEN. Listen, you don' have to say nothing. You just have to say "Ellen, you got too much of what the dog sniffs its arse with," and I'll hold me mouth. I won't take offence.

ANNIE. I was in service, oh, not round here, no, in a beautiful house in Blackheath, and I was real proud of meself, oh, I was. The master and mistress was all right, never thrashed you or anything, they was above that. Had a son at Oxford University, really nice spoken, educated gentleman. When he came home in the holiday, he wouldn't let me be. In front of anybody, I mean, he treated me like dirt, but would creep up on me when no one was about. I fought him. I pleaded with him, I threatened him, but he'd laugh. His mama would never believe it of her darling son. Oh, and I wasn't the only one, and it didn't only happen once and when I fell, that was it—got shot of me. I 'ad nowhere ter go, nowhere. I walked the streets and I was picked up and taken to be examined—six months gone I was—for diseases; to them I was a prostitute and the way they treat you and the way they look at you, and the way they hate you, and the way they blame you and everyone blames me. But I never cried, not one of them saw me cry and when I got to that home, it was awful but it was heaven. And even when I was told it was dead I never cried. Why don't they tell you birth is such an awful, bloody, terrible, painful thing. It was born with the cord round its neck. It had strangled itself the poor, poor, little tiny thing and I looked at it before they took it away and I thought, you lucky, lucky bastard, how much better if I'd have been born like that.

(SHE starts to sob for the first time since the baby was born. ELLEN looks at her and puts her arms round her and lets her cry.)

Scene 6

Fade to KATE and JIM.

JIM. What was Lady Helena talking to you lot for this morning?

KATE. She's set up some poxy club.

JIM. Where? Why don't we go there now 'stead of being out here by the river?

KATE. It's only for girls.

JIM. That's not fair.

KATE. You earn more than me.

JIM. So?

KATE. That's not fair either.

JIM. You've been listening to that Ellen. She's not right in the head.

KATE. Don't say that. She's been a good friend to me, you know it. I like her.

JIM. I wish we could get married now, then you wouldn't have to work there at all.

KATE. I'd have to work somewhere. We couldn't live off your money and I'm not taking in washing and ending up me veins all bulging like Maggie's ol' girl.

JIM. But when the children come along …

KATE. 'Ere, they was saying something today—umm—about sausage skins.

JIM. Katie. How could you? I'm not putting no sausage skin on my … fer no one. I'm really shocked at you, you've got jus' like them and you used to be real nice.

KATE. I am real nice ain't I, but if you think I'm going to spend me life working like a horse fer nothing you'd be better off marrying a horse.

JIM. I'd have to put a saddle and bridle on yer so as I could ride you down the street like a real gent.

KATE. (*Suddenly tightening her hold round his neck aggressively.*) What you talking about? I'd squash the breath outta yer.

JIM. (*Struggles.*) Leggo.

KATE. (*Laughs.*) Sorry.

JIM. Lucky none of the blokes could see me. They'd make mincemeat outta me.

KATE. You don't like working there either do you?

JIM. I hate it. To the others, it's just a job. They get used to it don't think about it—they're lucky. I don't seem to be able to get used to it.

KATE. Best just to try and think of something else. I do, except when we get the meat and it's still warm. That's horrible.

JIM. What do you think about, then?

KATE. Daydreams mostly, but then there's always quite a lot of chat.

JIM. You know what I dream about? Having a shop.

KATE. What, a bleeding butcher's shop?

JIM. No, a toy shop, with sweets, gobstoppers, lucky bags.

ANNIE. (*Joining in.*) And ballad sheets and jumping jacks.

JIM. And proper toys made of wood. I could make them.

KATE. And I could paint 'em.

JIM. But people like us don't get shops. I mean we don't know where to start.

KATE. 'Course we do. Look at Mrs. Jones in Prince Street, she turned her front parlour into a shop.

JIM. Didn't last long.

KATE. Only 'cos her old man come back to her.

JIM. We don't know enough about it.

KATE. We could find out.

JIM. That might be one of the things they tell yer at the club.

KATE. Oh, yeah, that and how to give yer profits back to Jesus.

Scene 7

Fade to MAGGIE and her mum, EADY, who is putting washing through a mangle.

MAGGIE. Evening, Mother. I brought you a bottle.

EADY. Par, if it's not enough your father spending all his waking hours in the alehouse, now you're at it as well.

MAGGIE. (*Opening her own bottle and taking a swig.*) You know you like one of an evening.

EADY. Look at you supping that like you was a man or something. Put it down and give me a hand.

MAGGIE. (*Does so.*) New girl started today.

EADY. (*Not at all interested.*) Mmm.

MAGGIE. (*Trying to gain her interest.*) Ellen's gone with her to find somewhere to live.

EADY. Mmm.

MAGGIE. She was living in that place in Ashmead Road.

EADY. She what? She's one of them sort then.

MAGGIE. Suppose she must be.

EADY. Disgusting.

MAGGIE. She ain't brazen or nothing.

EADY. What would you know, her sort seldom are brazen in front of women. Different story with the men though. That place where you work must be hell on earth. Come home stinking to high heaven, no wonder you can't get a man, no one could come within a mile of yer without keeling over.

MAGGIE. I don't want no man.

EADY. You what? What did you say?

MAGGIE. I don't want to finish up like you, do I? Eleven children and half as many miscarriages.

EADY. Shut your mouth.

MAGGIE. What do I want with that, eh?

EADY. Oh, you think when I was your age I thought I'd be spending the rest of me life being a drudge? That I wouldn't be able to have no sleep fer working, working, working, all day and half the night?

MAGGIE. Why did you then?

EADY. Did what?

MAGGIE. Become a drudge.

EADY. Because that's what's destined fer us, ain't it? Get married, have children, half kill yerself trying to mek ends meet, that's our lot. That's life and there's no denying it.

MAGGIE. It's not going to be my life.

EADY. Ha, that's what I used to say. You'll learn. Though I doubt if you'll learn too much off of them hussies down that hole where you work.

(THEY continue to work in silence.)

MAGGIE. Why d'you do it then—have children? The whole thing don't seem to give you no pleasure, nor comfort or no joy as I see it.

EADY. Because, because, there are no whys and wherefores, it's natural, it's what we was put here for, that's why. And if I'd dared to say to me mother half of what you say to me I'd have been hit into next week.

MAGGIE. But ...

EADY. Nothing else happen today then?

MAGGIE. Oh yes, Lady Helena dropped in to see us.

EADY. I know, don't I. Not that you'd ever tell me that. No, you relish your acquaintance with fallen women more. No, I heard it from Mrs. Know-all-know-nothing in Czar Street. So what did she want?

MAGGIE. For us to go to her silly club, to learn how to become decent wives and mothers, I suppose.

EADY. If she's putting herself out for you, least you can do is show willing. God knows you could do with some lessons on those topics.

MAGGIE. (*Sweetly.*) But I've learnt all I need to know about being a good mother from you.

Scene 8

Outside the shed, POLLY, MAGGIE, ELLEN and KATE have finished their lunch.

POLLY. At least we've been allowed to eat our sarnies outside, since old Helena graced us.

ELLEN. Oh, Gawd, if they told you lot to work eight days a week, standing on yer heads, I'm sure after a couple of months you'd be saying "It ain't that bad really."

POLLY. Pay attention everybody, the saviour of working girls is talking.

KATE. Horrible though her birth-place was, a mere back room in Butchers Row, ridiculed and scorned by the world she taught us how to be free.

ELLEN. One day …

MAGGIE. One day, we'll be queuing up to buy her latest book. "My Life's Work Amongst the Gut Girls of the Gutter."

ELLEN. You can laugh but—(*SHE is interrupted by Harry.*)

HARRY. Time to get back to work, girls. Not you Ellen. You can take over from Jim this afternoon.

ELLEN. That's not my job.

HARRY. He's needed in the slaughtering pens. (*To Ellen.*) Unless you don't want a job at all.

(*ELLEN goes.*)

KATE. What you made him do that for?

HARRY. Since when did I answer to you? 'Ere where's the other one?

POLLY. Gone to strain her greens, if you must know.

HARRY. It'll be such a relief when Lady Helena has finished with you lot. I can't wait till I've got a bunch of decent young ladies working for me.

MAGGIE. She ain't even starting with us never mind finishing so you can forget it.

HARRY. Not if old Cuttle-Smythe gets his way with the Guvnors. She's bent his ear good and proper. And, if and when he wins through, you'll all be enticed to attend soirees at that club every Thursday evening.

KATE. What you on about, Harry?

HARRY. That's for me to know and you to find out. (*HE turns, prances off.*) Yes, I'd be delighted to help you, sir. Charmed to make your acquaintance, sir. Anything you say, sir. Your wish is my command, sir.

(*ANNIE comes in.*)

ANNIE. What's he up to?

POLLY. Don't worry about him. He's just had a turn.

ANNIE. Where's Ellen?

KATE. She's doing Jim's job for the rest of today.

ANNIE. That ain't right.

MAGGIE. Oh, no, living in the same house as Ellen ain't done you no good at all girl. She's contaminated yer.

ANNIE. She's got good ideas she has.

POLLY. Her trouble is she prefers shouting to laughing.

MAGGIE. I mean who else d'you know who'd rather read a book than go to the Music Hall?

KATE. Don't talk about her when she's not here.

ANNIE. There is more to life than having a good time in the couple of hours they give you off at the end of a day.

POLLY. What you on about? You was only saying the other day how you was, now you're used to it like, happier than you been in yer life.

ANNIE. I am. I can choose what I do in the evenings, I don't have to clear up after other people. I've got enough money to pay me rent and still buy a new hat, and I got friends ...

KATE. So, what you moaning about?

ANNIE. It would be better, say, if we had a separate room to eat in, and wash our hands and a proper place to piss.

MAGGIE. You can't have everything you want in life, girl.

Scene 9

Outside Lady Helena's house. ARTHUR is exasperated by Priscilla's reluctance of mind. HE grabs hold of her elbow and turns her towards him.

ARTHUR. For God's sake Priscilla, anyone would think I was asking you to put your head in the lion's den. All I am asking is that you be nice to Lady Helena for my sake.

PRISCILLA. It's just that I don't ...

ARTHUR. I know you don't feel like it. I know you'd prefer to sit and stare out of the window all day. I know you don't feel cheerful but please at least act cheerful in front of her, don't show me up.

PRISCILLA. I don't want to let you down ...

ARTHUR. Then prove it. You're my wife, this is the chance to show your worth. I don't ask much of you, God knows. Just do this for me. She likes you. It's very important it stays that way. If we can become good friends of hers who knows where it will lead ...

PRISCILLA. But this club, I'm nervous Arthur, I don't think I'm cut out ...

ARTHUR. Just go along with her ideas, crackpot as they sound—for me.

PRISCILLA. But, I ...

ARTHUR. Try, woman, try. Try to be charming, enthusiastic and even vivacious. Don't you understand there's a lot riding on this for us. Don't throw it away.

PRISCILLA. I will try.

ARTHUR. That's it, please just look the part for me. Smile—that's better. Smile.

LADY HELENA. Priscilla, Arthur, how good of you to come.

ARTHUR. Priscilla is very excited at the prospect of helping you with your work.

PRISCILLA. It's just that I ...

ARTHUR. On the other matter, I have spoken to the girls' direct employers who have voiced, unfortunately, some concern over allowing the girls to leave an hour earlier on a Thursday. Mainly that it might encourage a lapse of punctuality, that sort of thing.

LADY HELENA. I can assure you that my aim is to help them lead more responsible lives.

ARTHUR. I know that. It's just if you were able to write to the employers yourself, telling them of your intentions, I'm sure they would comply.

LADY HELENA. Of course. I shall do that today.

ARTHUR. I'll leave you two ladies to plan your strategies in peace. Lady Helena. Priscilla. (*HE kisses Priscilla on the cheek. HE goes.*)

LADY HELENA. Such a charming man, your husband.

PRISCILLA. Mmm.

LADY HELENA. And I'm delighted that you are as excited about my little venture as I am.

PRISCILLA. It's just that …

LADY HELENA. Shall I ring for Emy and ask for tea?

PRISCILLA. No. Please don't bother on my account. Emy? Do you call your servants by their pet names?

LADY HELENA. I've taken to it quite recently. I can't see it does any harm. After all they are people too.

PRISCILLA. Do they not take liberties, become over-familiar?

LADY HELENA. Not at all. If I saw any sign of that, I should put a stop to it.

PRISCILLA. We have a great deal of trouble keeping parlourmaids in particular. There are so many households with vacancies, it seems servants can pick and choose where they go or what they want to do these days.

LADY HELENA. Quite so. But whilst choice is there for them, there is very little choice for those young women in the gutting sheds and they are the object of my concern. In fact it's high time I spoke to the MP for Deptford about them.

PRISCILLA. Ah, I was just about ...

LADY HELENA. I thought with your husband's interest in the place you might know something about them.

PRISCILLA. I have only one piece of information and I'm not sure how to impart it without giving offence.

LADY HELENA. Please speak freely. I need all the facts, however grimy.

PRISCILLA. Apparently they wear no undergarments at all.

LADY HELENA. None at all? (*Then.*) But they have such expensively vulgar hats.

PRISCILLA. Obviously they prefer to spend their money on outward frippery.

LADY HELENA. So that's something to be given priority on the club's agenda—sewing lessons.

PRISCILLA. But where do I come in?

LADY HELENA. Do you play the piano?

PRISCILLA. Why, yes.

LADY HELENA. Excellent. You shall be my right arm at the club.

PRISCILLA. Are you going to run the club yourself?

LADY HELENA. Just until it gathers momentum as it were. It seems the presence of my personality will pull the crowds. (*Laughs.*) As I'm sure yours will too, Priscilla dear.

PRISCILLA. Is that all you want of me? To play the piano?

LADY HELENA. Of course not. I wouldn't dream of patronising your capabilities. No, I have several other tasks allotted for you. One very important one you can do for me this evening.

PRISCILLA. Well that's just it ... I really don't feel...

LADY HELENA. I know, Priscilla. But sometimes, and please don't take this the wrong way, one needs help to overcome one's shyness.

PRISCILLA. Please don't mention doctors, I have quite lost faith in them.

LADY HELENA. I couldn't agree more. My run-ins with them have left a lot to be desired. They might have intricate brains, but the other parts of them are, more often than not, ham-fisted. No, Priscilla, we have to learn to help ourselves. And, what better way than to find an interest outside the confines of domesticity?

Scene 10

The Music Hall. The stage is occupied by MADJACKO. ANNIE, POLLY, KATE and MAGGIE enter with drinks.

MADJACKO. Thank you ladies and gentlemen, thank you very much for a warm welcome. I always look forward to coming back here to the Empire in Deptford.

MAGGIE. Me mum didn't half kick up a stink about me going out again—(*Calls out in Madjacko's direction.*) it'd better be worth it.

KATE. Stop moaning.

MADJACKO. You're a friendly couple. You're honoured you are. You know the place you reside in is named after you—the people. Deptford. Everyone's in debt for things they can't afford. It's a hard life. Debt. Don't talk to me about debt. I'm up to here I am. (*Holds hand under chin.*) Wish I was a bit taller. That ferry service you got. Yes, that's right, what service. A man can go mad waiting for that to take him across the river. Saw this fella only yesterday. Given up, walking towards me down the High street going like this. (*Mimes rowing.*) I said "Excuse me mate, but you ain't got no boat." He says "Haven't I? Jesus Christ" and he starts going like this. (*Mimes swimming.*) I said "Don't worry mate, you'll soon be walking under the water." He gave me an old-fashioned look. But yer soon to get a new foot tunnel at Greenwich. Isn't that right?

ANNIE. What is he—a sort of speaking newspaper?

POLLY. Only less entertaining.

MADJACKO. But you'll be taking your picnics and your days out on the Isle of Dogs once the tunnel's built. And talking of dogs, you got your own isle of them up the top of the road here. Except none of 'em, to my knowledge, have ever walked up an aisle.

KATE. Guess what's coming next?

MAGGIE. Let him try ...

POLLY. Shut up, Mag.

ANNIE. What? What's coming next?

MADJACKO. The gut girls. Now if you take one of
them home, boys … the dog sits in the corner biting its
nails. You gotta watch them, fellas. Hard as nails they are,
and drink? Drink, they ain't got hair on their chests they
got twigs. Crack your ribs they could—with their eyelids.
Oh, but they're being well looked after. Did you know
they've even got their own patron saint—St. Nickerless.
He has to keep an eye on 'em on account of they don't
wear none. And no one wants to marry a girl like that I can
tell yer. But if that weren't enough, oh my, now the
Duchess has taken 'em under her wing, going to give 'em
all a new pedigree.

(PRISCILLA enters.)

POLLY. Bleedin' hell, that's old Cuttle-Smythe's wife.
MAGGIE. Never mind her, fix yer eye on laughing
Jacko there.
MADJACKO. *(Turning his attention to Priscilla.)*
What's this then—a charity walk? *(PRISCILLA stops, like
a frightened rabbit.)* You must have got the wrong address,
lady. Don't you want the Temperance Society?
(PRISCILLA stands still.) Where do you come from? *(No
response.)* Don't keep us all in suspense, where you from?
PRISCILLA. *(Timidly.)* Brockley.
MADJACKO. Brockley … umm nice place … bit like
Lee Green with rigor mortis … No. No, nice place to come
from … Not a nice place to go, mind. Do you do good
works, lady? No need to be shy I bet you do. Well, see
there was this Christian lady, this woman from the
humanitarian league and this gut girl …
POLLY. *(Shouts.)* We can't hear yer.

MAGGIE. (*Shouts.*) All we can feel is a draught.

KATE. What's got four legs, a tail and barks?

MADJACKO. A dog.

ANNIE. So you do know what dogs are then.

MADJACKO. You lot got a sister called Cinderella.

MAGGIE. Just 'cos you look like someone sat on yer whilst you were still hot.

KATE. You're so ugly, when you were born the midwife slapped yer mother.

POLLY. They warned us if we chopped up bacon a pig would come back and haunt us—and it's here tonight.

MADJACKO. (*He can no longer be heard over the sound of the girls and decides to beat a retreat.*) Thank you ladies and gentlemen, thank you very much. Goodnight.

ANNIE. Good riddance.

MAGGIE. Let's go round the back and get him.

POLLY. (*Bringing her back.*) Leave it Mag ... Oh blimey don't look now.

MAGGIE. What?

KATE. Only Ma Cuttle-Smythe.

ANNIE. She's coming over to us.

KATE. What a show up.

MAGGIE. Don't let her see us fer Christ's sake. We'll never live it down.

(*PRISCILLA bravely picks her way towards them as THEY try to look away or hide under the table.*)

PRISCILLA. Good evening.

MAGGIE. (*Emerging awkwardly from under the table.*) Evening miss.

POLLY. Can I get yer a drink?

PRISCILLA. No err, thank you. It's just, I'm here ...

KATE. Why don't yer sit down and take the weight off yer pins.

PRISCILLA. Again, thank you, but Lady Helena, has asked me to come here to let you know that she herself is at the club this evening, and to persuade you to come along.

ANNIE. But we've paid to get in here.

POLLY. Now if Lady Helena were to come down here and do a turn up there on the stage we'd all be happy.

PRISCILLA. Please say you will.

MAGGIE. I'm sorry but look this is our time and surely we can spend it as we please?

PRISCILLA. Yes, of course. But I'm sure that in the long run the club will be of more benefit to you.

POLLY. We're happy where we is, thanks.

PRISCILLA. Well, if you change your mind, you know ...

ALL. Creek Road.

PRISCILLA. Yes. (*SHE turns and walks away.*)

KATE. What are we going to do?

MAGGIE. What we always do when someone tells us what we should be doing—take no bleeding notice.

KATE. What's so special about this place? At least Lady Helena won't stand around insulting us.

MAGGIE. Par, she'll have to come up with better enticement than that if she wants me to go to her bleedin' club.

(*But KATE stands up.*)

ACT II

Scene 1

*The club is in complete contrast to the shed. It is clean,
clinical, sparse and quiet. POLLY, KATE, ANNIE and
MAGGIE sit, sewing knickers for themselves.*

LADY HELENA. Quiet please. (*The room falls to
hush. LADY HELENA goes over to Priscilla.*)
PRISCILLA. It was an excellent idea to allow them to
leave work an hour early. The place is full to overflowing
every week.
LADY HELENA. Unfortunately, the majority of them
are still extremely unwilling to learn. Immediate
gratification is the name of their game. Can't see the value
of what they will achieve in the long run.
PRISCILLA. Give them a few more weeks.
LADY HELENA. But in the meantime. I'm afraid of
losing their interest so I've asked Edwin to pop in with a
surprise.
PRISCILLA. Oh?

*(While LADY HELENA and PRISCILLA have their backs
turned the GIRLS start to whisper to each other.)*

ANNIE. I can't understand Ellen. Still not coming here,
even with an hour off.

MAGGIE. Except that we have to stay for three hours in total and it's worse than school.

KATE. It's not hard work though is it?

MAGGIE. At least me Mum don't give me no aggravation 'bout coming here. She's well pleased me and Lady Helena are breathing the same air. What's the matter with you Pol, lost yer tongue?

POLLY. I'm trying to finish me fucking knickers ain't I?

ANNIE. What's so special 'bout your fanny?

MAGGIE. Annie, really. Try and remember you're a young lady.

KATE. Here Polly, I dare you to call Lady Helena, Lena.

POLLY. I dare you to try her hat on.

KATE. Call that a hat, looks more like a frozen cow turd.

LADY HELENA. Girls, girls, your attention please, you are here to learn not chatter.

MAGGIE. (*To the others.*) Wait for it, she's now going to make up a new rule.

ANNIE. D'you remember the first time, when she said there'd be no rules.

KATE. Yeah, now there's about twenty.

LADY HELENA. I will not tolerate talking whilst I'm talking, it is extremely bad manners.

POLLY. Look, miss, I've finished. (*SHE holds up an enormous pair of bloomers with about eight pockets, all shaped like pork chops or some recognisable piece of meat.*)

MAGGIE. Creep.

LADY HELENA. (*Walking over to her.*) We usually wait till we're asked but (*Looking at the knickers.*) you have done well. I didn't expect anyone to finish until next week at least. Are you sure they're not a little on the large side? And, good gracious me, all these pockets. What on earth?

POLLY. Hankies, miss. We need a lot of them. Don't do ter go wiping yer nose on yer hand. Knife would slip right outta it.

LADY HELENA. Now where was I?

POLLY. Oh, Lena.

LADY HELENA. I beg your pardon.

POLLY. (*Holds up the knickers.*) You meant I was leaner. I've made these too big. Was that what you was meaning?

LADY HELENA. Oh I see. (*Looking at Polly.*) It is quite possible I was mistaken. Now I would like, with your consent of course, to introduce a new rule.

KATE. (*To Polly.*) Dare you to call her Hell then.

POLLY. Give over, you got to try her hat on first.

LADY HELENA. (*Talking over them.*) This new rule is that no loose women should be allowed to come to the club.

KATE. We don't know what you mean, Mam.

MAGGIE. (*To Annie.*) Don't worry, we won't say nothing. Don't say nothing.

POLLY. I know I could be leaner but (*Holding up her arm.*) this is all muscle. May look loose but honest, miss, it's muscle.

LADY HELENA. Those who have strayed from the path of virtue.

MAGGIE. Which side of Evelyn Street is that on?

LADY HELENA. I meant fallen women.

POLLY. (*Trips and falls on the floor.*) Oh blimey, what am I going to do, I've fallen.

(*The OTHERS slip off their chairs.*)

MAGGIE. Oh no, we're all fallen women.

LADY HELENA. That's quite enough. All of you get up this instant, put your sewing away and sit, hands in laps. It's time for the Bible reading. (*SHE opens the Bible trying to find her place.*) Ah, here we are. Now I've found something very relevant and something I think you'll find very interesting because it's directly connected to St. Nicholas's church which is the church just around the corner from where you work. Now who can tell me what it's got on its gate posts?

MAGGIE. (*Mutters.*) Dog shit.

KATE. (*Calls out.*) Two skulls.

LADY HELENA. Quite right. And does anyone know why?

POLLY. (*Calls out.*) Two heads is better than one, miss?

LADY HELENA. That's as may be, but these two have biblical significance. Can anyone tell me what it is?

MAGGIE. (*Calls out.*) To remind us that there's more dead people in the world than live ones.

LADY HELENA. In fact not, no. They resemble a vision Ezekiel was given by God. And I'm going to read it to you. Now the language is rather antiquated and cumbersome so bear with me whilst I paraphrase for your benefit.

ANNIE. (*Mutters.*) Wake me up when it's time to go to the pub.

(LADY HELENA has to look down to do this. Consequently SHE can't see them ALL messing about. KATE immediately gets up stands behind her, puts her hat on and starts mimicking.)

LADY HELENA. Ezekiel, Chapter 47. I felt the powerful presence of the Lord. He took me to the valley of dry bones. He said to me, "Can these bones come back to life?" I replied, "Lord only you can answer that." He said, "Tell these dry bones to listen to the work of God. Tell them I am the sovereign Lord," and thus said the Lord God "behold I will come, breathe life into you and you shall live. I will give you muscles and cover you with skin and cause your blood to flow."

(KATE quickly replaces the hat, the GIRLS applaud.)

LADY HELENA. I'm pleased you enjoyed that, but we don't usually clap at the Bible. Still I particularly like that passage myself.

MAGGIE. Oh miss, excuse me, but where we come from "passage" is a rude word.

LADY HELENA. Can anyone tell me what it means.

KATE. Well, it's like your "underneath": yer privates.

LADY HELENA. No. The reading from the Bible, can anyone tell me what they think the significance is.

POLLY. Hell?

LADY HELENA. What did you say?

POLLY. Isn't it like a vision of hell, everything dried up and that.

LADY HELENA. Oh I see. Yes, well done, Polly. It is sort of but with a happy ending and shall I tell you why I like it?

MAGGIE. (*Mumbles.*) Do we have the power to stop you?

LADY HELENA. Because it's what I see today in Deptford. Young people like yourselves, all dried up without hope and future. But it doesn't have to be like that.

MAGGIE. (*Mutters.*) Bleedin' arrogance of the silly mare.

POLLY. Maybe she means the sheep girls.

MAGGIE. I don't care who she means. If anybody needs to dry up should be her.

LADY HELENA. Now next week is Holy Week.

KATE. (*To Maggie.*) No such luck.

LADY HELENA. Who knows what Holy Week is about?

MAGGIE. Having a good time.

LADY HELENA. It is not. It is remembering that Jesus died and suffered for each and everyone of us. But ...

POLLY. Who?

LADY HELENA. Our Lord, Jesus Christ.

MAGGIE. Never heard of him.

(*Chorus of "No."*)

KATE. Yes, you have. They're being silly miss. We learnt it at school, he was the one what gave someone a kiss.

LADY HELENA. Well, I can't quite recall.

POLLY. Nelson, that's right.

LADY HELENA. Goodness me, that's .... Come on now you must know who. (*SHE sees Edwin come in.*) Excuse me a moment.

ANNIE. (*To the others.*) Don't keep this up. Now we'll get the life story of Jesus.

MAGGIE. (*To Annie.*) I wouldn't fret. We was going to get it anyway.

LADY HELENA. Listen, listen. This evening we have a special treat. Something that I'm sure will amaze you. Lord Tartaden very kindly agreed to come along with a lantern slide and we will be able to see details from our Lord's life with the aid of magic.

(*EDWIN sets it up. The GIRLS show genuine interest for the first time, never having seen a lantern show before, it must seem like magic to them.*)

EDWIN. All set.

LADY HELENA. Perhaps you'd be so good as to take us through.

EDWIN. (*Decides to charm the girls by being skittish.*) Right ho. (*Picture of Jesus in the manger.*) Here we have a picture of Jesus in the first perambulator ever invented. It wasn't until some years later that they decided to put wheels on it.

LADY HELENA. (*Hisses.*) This is supposed to be educational, Edwin. (*Then to the girls.*) This picture shows that the Son of God started life in very humble surroundings.

EDWIN. Here we have spouting—er—teaching in the temple, aged twelve. Then a little gap in the story 'til we

find him here on the cross. (*Picture of the crucifixion.*)
What a way to spend Easter eh?

LADY HELENA. He died so that we might know too
of the life hereafter, to let us know that we all have a
choice here on earth to be born again, a fresh start. Lord
Tartaden, do you have the picture of the stone being rolled
away?

EDWIN. Umm, let's see now. Oh yes, well, there's one
of him making his first public appearance after the
crucifixion to old Mary Magdalene.

LADY HELENA. Ah, now she is a very important
character, and one of my favourites amongst the women in
the New Testament. This Mary, unlike the mother of God,
was shunned by those around her. She was coarse and led a
heathen, contemptuous way of life, but Jesus didn't judge
her. He went out of His way to get to know her and
through Him her life was completely transformed.

MAGGIE. (*To others.*) What's she getting at?

ANNIE. (*Shrugs.*) Search me.

LADY HELENA. Now please dismiss quietly, and
remember to behave with social manners, not only whilst
in this room but in the street, and in your work. This week
I want you to take our Lord Jesus home with you. I'll see
you all next week at eight o'clock prompt.

(*THEY start to put their hats and coats on. EDWIN goes
over to Helena and helps her on with her coat.*)

POLLY. (*Unseen, except by Maggie, carefully takes the
slide of Jesus and puts it in her coat pocket.*) Come on
Jesus.

MAGGIE. (*Hisses.*) What you doing?

POLLY. (*Shrugs.*) She said we had to tek Jesus home with us.

MAGGIE. C'mon, let's get outta here.

(THEY all rush out laughing, screaming and shouting.)

LADY HELENA. (*Sighs, puts her hand to her forehead.*) Little more than riotous beasts.

EDWIN. (*With enthusiasm.*) Rather. (*Then.*) I mean high-spirited coltishness.

LADY HELENA. Magic lantern was a great success. Many thanks, Tarty.

EDWIN. Don't mention it. I must be off. (*HE kisses her on the cheek.*)

LADY HELENA. Edwin.

EDWIN. Wishful thinking, wishful thinking. (*HE goes.*)

LADY HELENA. Well, Priscilla, we certainly have our work cut out.

PRISCILLA. (*Collects the undergarments.*) There's one pair missing.

LADY HELENA. That one, Polly, finished hers. I was quite astounded. She shows precious little interest in anything else.

PRISCILLA. But she hasn't paid for them.

LADY HELENA. We'll see her next week. Don't worry. Maybe we should try and extend the activities of the sewing class. Poor children have such disgusting clothes.

PRISCILLA. That awful, gaudy jewellery and those hideous hats.

Scene 2

In the street.

MAGGIE. What I can't understand is them having all that money and wearing such awful clothes.

POLLY. That hat. Fancy wearing it. I wouldn't be caught dead being seen in something like that in the street.

KATE. If she'd'ave caught me wearing it I'd only be half alive.

ANNIE. I ain't going next week.

MAGGIE. Listen Annie, don't take it to heart, that rubbish about fallen women. She don't know anything 'bout yer and she ain't going ter find out neither.

ANNIE. But that ain't the point is it. Anyway, I can't work out what she's bothering with us for in the first place.

POLLY. She wants to turn us into real ladies, don't she.

MAGGIE. You lot are getting as bad as old po-faced Ellen, you are. And I've got to get home, otherwise I'll get it off old misery chops.

POLLY. She ain't that bad, yer Mum.

MAGGIE. You don't know her like I do.

ANNIE. We'll walk yer to the bottom of Evelyn Street.

MAGGIE. Don't worry, I'm not so much of a lady yet to be worried about a few drunks. See yer tomorrow.

POLLY. Night.

(MAGGIE walks on alone. SHE thinks she can hear something. Looks back. Nothing there. Walks on.

EDWIN suddenly steps out of the shadows blocking her path.)

EDWIN. Good evening, young lady.

MAGGIE. (*Levelly.*) Evening, sir. (*SHE steps to one side. HE steps in front of her. SHE looks at him.*) Mind if I get on me way?

EDWIN. You've got time to stop and talk with a gentleman, just for a while, haven't you?

MAGGIE. No, please let me pass.

EDWIN. (*Takes her arm.*) How would you like to earn a shilling?

MAGGIE. (*Removes his hand. Nervous.*) Don't touch what you can't afford, sir.

EDWIN. Oh, but I can afford anything I want.

MAGGIE. I just want to get home. Please get out of my way.

EDWIN. I only want a few moments of your time.

MAGGIE. I said no sir, now.

EDWIN. (*Pushing her. Suddenly produces a small pocket knife and points it at her.*) Now this is not the way I normally like to conduct business, but you leave me very little option.

MAGGIE. (*Steps back. Looks at him.*) I work all day with these. (*SHE gracefully pulls out a large knife from her skirts.*) So don't make me laugh wiv that plaything. (*SHE brings her knife down and knocks it from his hand.*) And if you don't want ter see yer wedding tackle on sale in Wellbeloved's tomorrow—fer less than a shilling no doubt—I'd scarper and sharpish (*Prods him.*) mate.

EDWIN. (*Backing off.*) I'll get you for this, you slut. Don't think I don't know who you are, where you work. I'll find yer. Next time darling, next time.

(*HE goes. SHE watches him. HE breaks into a run. SHE into a sweat.*)

Scene 3

LADY HELENA at the club. PRISCILLA enters, SHE has a bruise on her face which SHE has tried to conceal with powder. HELENA doesn't notice until SHE looks closely.

LADY HELENA. Priscilla, so prompt, as always. Lovely to see you. I have just finished the revised agenda for next Thursday. Have you brought your music?

PRISCILLA. Yes. (*SHE takes out a pile of sheet music.*)

LADY HELENA. Your face. Goodness what on earth's happened?

PRISCILLA. Oh nothing. Really. It looks worse than it is. I thought I'd try. (*SHE shows the music to Helena.*)

LADY HELENA. It looks frightful.

PRISCILLA. Sorry?

LADY HELENA. Not the music. Your face.

PRISCILLA. Oh, Helena, I walked into a door. Very clumsy and very stupid. Serves me right for wandering round in the dark, tripped and banged myself. I'm quite all right, thank you.

LADY HELENA. Are you sure?

PRISCILLA. Perfectly. Now let me ...

LADY HELENA. I hope Arthur has been looking after you.

PRISCILLA. Yes, yes, he has.

LADY HELENA. He is such a thoughtful man.

PRISCILLA. Yes, he is, he is. He's a good man. He is.

LADY HELENA. Without his help and concern we wouldn't have such a success on our hands.

PRISCILLA. He's tried his best, it's been very difficult for him. You have to try and see his point of view. (*SHE starts to cry.*)

LADY HELENA. (*Both concerned and embarrassed by this display of emotion.*) I'm sure, I'm sure. Please, Priscilla, don't upset yourself.

PRISCILLA. It's not for me I'm upset you understand, it's for him really. He's quite distraught and I've been no help whatsoever.

LADY HELENA. He's distraught? Because you bump into things?

PRISCILLA. No, no I'm afraid it's all come as rather a shock to him.

LADY HELENA. Priscilla dear, please take a deep breath and tell me what all this is about.

PRISCILLA. Arthur is displeased about the girls.

LADY HELENA. But he seemed so agreeable to the idea of the club. Why he even ...

PRISCILLA. No that, no, about them having to be laid off next month.

LADY HELENA. What? Why?

PRISCILLA. Because a large amount of his capital is tied up in those sheds.

LADY HELENA. Yes, yes. But why are they being laid off?

PRISCILLA. Oh something to do with the Corporation of London. Stopping imports. I'm afraid I didn't fully understand.

LADY HELENA. This is absolutely terrible.

PRISCILLA. But I thought, we both did, that it was your doing. I mean didn't you say that you thought it should be made illegal for girls to work there?

LADY HELENA. But this is too soon. Much too soon. Those girls are unemployable elsewhere. Besides I haven't even had time to take the tea with the MP of Deptford, never mind chivvy legislation.

PRISCILLA. You didn't know anything about it?

LADY HELENA. This is the first I'd heard of it. It's disastrous. Those girls have no skills whatsoever. I must go to the Corporation today and beg them, yes, beg them if necessary, to reverse their decision.

PRISCILLA. But I think it's all cut and dried.

LADY HELENA. At the very least I will request an extension of time.

PRISCILLA. Would you like me to come with you?

LADY HELENA. No, you go home and rest, and set poor Arthur's mind at rest too.

Scene 4

The sheds. There seems very little work for them.

MAGGIE. Makes me bleedin' laugh it does. All that gab about fallen women. And then that bastard starts on me in the street. Threatening me and all sorts. That's it, I ain't going near that poxy club again.

KATE. You should tell her, Lady Helena, what happened. Don't let him get away with it.

POLLY. And who's she going to believe? Between Maggie and him? It'll be him every time.

ANNIE. You know what they should do, don't yer— pull their cocks off. They'd only have to do it to one. That would make all the others stop and think "Now do I really want to rape this woman or do I want my cock pulled off."

KATE. Blimey, you've changed.

MAGGIE. And I'm sick to the back teeth of these toffs waltzing through here, saying how awful it is—it's them by calling it awful made it seem so awful.

KATE. It's always been awful. It's not just them saying it. This is an awful job whoever has to do it.

ANNIE. But one thing's for sure. It'll never be the likes of Lady Helena, doing it.

POLLY. (*Picks up some sheeps ribs and puts them round her waist.*) And the sovereign lord said unto me "Lady Hell, gather up them dead bones and put 'em round yer body so they squash the living daylights outta yer."

ANNIE. Watch it, Pol. Don't let Harry catch yer.

POLLY. I just had a vision. I was in the valley of dry bones. Make haste and take me ...

(ELLEN comes in.)

MAGGIE. Carry on, Pol. It's only Ellen.

ANNIE. (*To Ellen.*) What are you doing here? I thought Harry put you on unloading again.

ELLEN. He has. Listen. Listen ... I just sneaked back ... I just heard we're all going to be laid off.

POLLY. (*Picks her up swings her around.*) Oh, you just had a vision an' all?

ELLEN. *(Angry.)* No, no. This isn't a joke.

KATE. How d'you know then?

MAGGIE. Probably something Jasper found out from his father's friends in the city.

ANNIE. When?

ELLEN. I don't know exactly know. But I overheard these two chaps.

POLLY. Ellen, you should know by now they'd do anything to wind us up.

(HARRY comes in.)

HARRY. Ellen what in hell's name are you doing in here? Get back up to the river end and count yerself lucky I've not fired you. (*ELLEN goes.*) Which one of you ain't going to the club tonight to play pretty miss with Lady Helena?

MAGGIE. Rest assured, Harry, I ain't setting foot in that place ever again.

HARRY. Right, you go out there and help Ellen. We need all the help we can get this evening.

(MAGGIE goes.)

ANNIE. What's going on, Harry?

HARRY. (*Sincerely.*) I don't know, girls, really I don't. They don't tell me anything. (*HARRY goes.*)

POLLY. Scaremongering again. The same happened two years back, when all the cattle got ill on the voyage over here but we're still here ain't we.

ANNIE. Why, then did Harry ... ?

POLLY. 'Cos he likes to wind us up. Here why don't we get our own back on him—I've still got that Jesus picture. Let's shine it up on the wall an' Harry will believe Jesus has come to take him off to heaven.

ANNIE. What good would that do?

POLLY. I dunno. Be a laugh though.

KATE. You gotta put it in that special light box and you ain't got one, you dozy gizzard.

ANNIE. Ellen's telling us that we ain't going to have no jobs and all you can think about is having a laugh.

POLLY. How can we not have any jobs? They've even taken some of us away to unload the ships, there are that many beasts.

ANNIE. So how come the sheds are so empty?

KATE. 'Cos there's always a delay—getting them slaughtered and that before they come into the sheds.

POLLY. And they need us to clean out the innards. Now all animals have got insides whatever Lady Helena or Ellen may think. So until they find a beast without none, we'll always have a job.

KATE. You're right. But I reckon we'd be best keeping in with Lady Helena just to be on the safe side.

POLLY. Let's stop off at yours first Annie, and have a quick supper.

ANNIE. But we ain't got nothing.

POLLY. (*Lifting up her skirts to reveal the pockets stuffed with cuts of meat.*) The Lord will provide.

Scene 5

The club. HELENA and NORA (one of Helena's servants who works below stairs).

LADY HELENA. Nora, would you get the caps and aprons ready?

NORA. Very good, madam. (*SHE proceeds to make a collection of caps and aprons from a bag, smooth them out and put them over the chair.*)

(PRISCILLA comes in.)

LADY HELENA. Priscilla, you got my message, how good of you to come a bit earlier.

PRISCILLA. Have you heard anything from the Corporation?

LADY HELENA. Oh, your face. It's better.

PRISCILLA. Yes, it was nothing.

LADY HELENA. No joy at all I'm afraid. From the Corporation. Nothing I could do or say would change their minds.

PRISCILLA. Oh, but that's terrible.

LADY HELENA. I thought so too. But then, when I really sat down and thought it through I said to myself "It doesn't have to look so bleak." Isn't this the Godsent opportunity we were waiting for? There isn't time for despondency we must use the time we have got to the full.

PRISCILLA. But they …

LADY HELENA. They will have to work hard and be pushed for their own benefit.

(KATE, ANNIE and POLLY arrive, chatting and laughing.)

PRISCILLA. I've brought the music you ...

LADY HELENA. I don't think we'll be needing it. From now on Priscilla, it's got to be work and not much play. Otherwise these girls will be on the street. *(Raising her voice to be heard.)* Settle down girls please. There isn't room for slackers, it isn't fair on those who want to learn.

KATE. *(Pointing at Nora.)* Here, who's her?

LADY HELENA. Who can tell me what was wrong with that statement? *(Silence.)* Firstly we never point. It is extremely rude. Secondly, the correct way of phrasing the question is "Excuse me, but who is that young lady?"

KATE. Well, who is she then?

LADY HELENA. Thirdly, one doesn't speak until one is spoken to. *(Then.)* Nora, is what's called an undermaid, in my household.

POLLY. *(Mutters.)* Under the thumb.

LADY HELENA. If you want to mumble or pass comments under your breath then you'd better go outside and do it. I have brought Nora along as an example of what you might aspire to if you listen carefully and learn quickly. If you don't want to, then are plenty of others willing to take your place. Nora will you stand here next to me.

(NORA stands, legs together, back straight, looking impassively in front of her.)

KATE. (*To Annie.*) Do you think she knows something we don't?

ANNIE. Best not to fall out with her now, that's what I think.

LADY HELENA. All of you separate yourselves, so you don't feel tempted to chat. Now what do you notice about Nora?

POLLY. She ain't said nothing.

LADY HELENA. She hasn't said anything. Repeat after me. She hasn't said anything.

POLLY. (*Begrudgingly.*) She hasn't said anything.

LADY HELENA. You see you can talk properly when you want to. Why hasn't she said anything? No don't answer that it's a rhetorical question. She hasn't said anything because we do not speak until we are spoken to. And when we do answer, we do so as precisely and politely as possible.

KATE. Do what?

LADY HELENA. What have I just said?

POLLY. She don't know, that's why she's asking.

LADY HELENA. No-one speaks until they are spoken to, isn't that correct, Nora?

NORA. Yes, madam.

LADY HELENA. Thank you. Now I want you to look at Nora very carefully. She is extremely well groomed. Her cap and apron, impeccably starched and stain free. You do not wipe dirty hands on your apron. Your appearance is all important. Nora would you please show these young ladies how to enter a room correctly. Mrs. Cuttle-Smythe and I shall pretend to take afternoon tea.

(SHE and PRISCILLA sit down.)

LADY HELENA. Would you care to take tea with me this afternoon, Mrs. Cuttle-Smythe?

PRISCILLA. I should be delighted Lady Helena.

LADY HELENA. I shall ring for Nora. *(Ringing the hand bell)*

(NORA enters.)

LADY HELENA. Ah, Nora, would you bring tea for Mrs. Cuttle-Smythe and myself. *(SHE hands Nora a tray.)*

NORA. Very good, madam.

(NORA goes out, comes back in with the tray, puts it on the table and pours tea from a pretend pot into pretend cups. POLLY, KATE and ANNIE make appropriate noises "tea pouring," sugar lumps plopping, and an enormous slurping sound as LADY HELENA and PRISCILLA pretend to take a sip.)

LADY HELENA. That will be all.

NORA. Thank you, madam.

LADY HELENA. *(Coming out of the charade.)* Now, what did you notice about Nora? *(Silence.)* That she carried herself in a ladylike manner, she took small steps not large strides, she stood with her back straight, didn't slouch her shoulders. She was alert and attentive at all times without being intrusive. Nora would you sit in this chair for me.

(NORA does so.)

LADY HELENA. Rarely will you be required to sit in your employer's presence but nevertheless it is important to sit in a ladylike manner at all times, even when you are alone. You sit with your back straight, your legs firmly together and your hands in your lap. Is that understood? Excellent Nora, well done. In real life, Nora has probably never seen inside my drawing room, certainly she has never served tea. That's because she works downstairs. But what is your ambition Nora?

NORA. To be head maid, madam.

LADY HELENA. And one day, I think, you're likely to achieve it. (*To the girls.*) Although you'll all be required to start at the bottom, it is worth remembering that domestic service gives you the chance to learn and improve so that when someone in a position above yours leaves to get married, there is every chance these days for promotion from within a household. Now that's enough talking. Please take your positions in a dignified manner, whilst Mrs. Cuttle-Smythe finds caps and aprons for you to try on and let's get down to the real work.

POLLY. (*To Annie.*) Oh my Gawd, she's going to dress us up as dollies.

LADY HELENA. In silence please. The next young lady I hear blaspheming, cursing or swearing, can leave. If you want to behave like street urchins then perhaps the street is the best place for you.

(*PRISCILLA fits them with caps and aprons.*)

LADY HELENA. What do you think Mrs. Cuttle-Smythe?

PRISCILLA. Well (*Straightening Polly's cap.*) with one or two adjustments.

LADY HELENA. (*To the girls.*) Take a look at Nora and then at yourselves. A tidy appearance denotes a tidy mind. A slovenly appearance is the outward sign of a slovenly mind. Walk across the room now in a ladylike manner, turn, come back to me and say "You rang, madam?" and remember all of you are capable of being young ladies, it is up to you.

(THEY set off across the room.)

LADY HELENA. (*To Priscilla*) What do you think?

PRISCILLA. Well ...

LADY HELENA. Don't forget, they all start with the most menial jobs. The sort they probably have to do at home for themselves now. It's the manner, appearance and attitude we have to break them into. (*Calls to the girls.*) Don't rush. Keep your heads up. No, not your noses in the air. Look ahead not down. Good, now turn round come back to me.

(THEY do so.)

GIRLS. (*Loudly.*) You rang, madam?

LADY HELENA. Not so loud. Don't drawl. Now one at a time. You.

ANNIE. You rang, madam?

LADY HELENA. Good.

ANNIE. I have been in service before.

LADY HELENA. (*Interrupting.*) No, no. I've not asked you a question. That'll be all. Go back and do it again. You.

POLLY. You rang, madam?

LADY HELENA. (*Pleasantly.*) There's a hint of impatience in your voice. Again.

POLLY. You rang, madam?

LADY HELENA. Better, you.

KATE. You rang, madam?

LADY HELENA. That sounds downright impertinent, again.

KATE. You rang, madam.

LADY HELENA. Again.

KATE. You rang, madam.

LADY HELENA. Not quite, go back and do it again. Don't look at one another. Don't frown. You don't want lines on your faces before you're thirty. No, well, come on. No, don't skip. All right, now Nora would you take the tray and mime bringing it in, pretending to open the door, set it on the table, and say "Will that be all, madam?"

NORA. Very good, madam.

(*SHE proceeds to do as she's told.*)

LADY HELENA. Now please would you follow Nora's example.

(*HELENA and PRISCILLA proceed to have their own private conversation punctuated by HELENA calling out instructions to the girls.*)

LADY HELENA. (*To Priscilla.*) Now, we're only going to put ourselves out for those girls who have attended the club regularly.

NORA. (*Having completed the mime.*) Will that be all, madam?

LADY HELENA. Thank you, Nora. Right, first one, off you go.

(*KATE goes first.*)

LADY HELENA. No, I don't think so. The tea service would have fallen from the tray by now, go back and start again. (*KATE does so. HELENA turns to Priscilla.*) Otherwise we're going to be inundated with requests for work and we must be seen to reward those girls who have made the club priority for Thursday evenings.

PRISCILLA. What about those absent because of sickness?

KATE. Will that be all, madam?

LADY HELENA. (*To Kate.*) Don't fidget, when you've poured the tea, stand up straight. Go back and do it once more. (*KATE passes the tray to POLLY. HELENA to Priscilla.*) If they are going to be sick then they won't make good employees. I've put the word out about finding work and I'm fairly confident that we'll only be left with a minority of disobedient, insolent girls that nobody with the best will in the world could do anything with. (*SHE sees POLLY bending over the tea table.*) Bend your knees slightly. Nobody wants the sight of your rear end taking up space in their drawing rooms.

POLLY. (*Straightening herself.*) Will that be all, madam?

LADY HELENA. Try again.

(ANNIE takes her turn.)

ANNIE. Will that be all, madam?

LADY HELENA. Very good. The rest of you would do well to follow this example.

PRISCILLA. It's quite extraordinary the amount of households now needing more servants.

ANNIE. *(To Polly.)* The sheep girls who work nights have been laid off.

LADY HELENA. You still need a maid yourself, don't you?

PRISCILLA. True.

LADY HELENA. Well, my dear, take your pick, if you can't have first choice after all the work you've put in I don't know who can. That last one was very good.

PRISCILLA. Do you know I rather like that one, Polly.

LADY HELENA. The girl who was so deft with the underwear? She's a bit dense. Not to mention ungainly.

PRISCILLA. But pleasingly gentle of temperament. Not like the others. She's very slow to take offence.

LADY HELENA. Right girls, let's do it again. *(To Priscilla.)* I think the coffee and cake will be well earned this evening.

(The GIRLS go through the routine again.)

PRISCILLA. I'll go and put the kettle on. *(SHE goes.)*

LADY HELENA. Hands by your sides, backs straight. Try at all times to look pleasant.

(The GIRLS go through the routine again)

POLLY. Will that be all, madam?
ANNIE. Very good, madam.
KATE. Thank you, madam.

Scene 6

HARRY, having given JIM his cards, sees him off the premises.

JIM. I thought I was going to be all right. I mean I thought it was just the girls what was laid off.

HARRY. I'm sorry, son. I am really. But nobody told me they was going to slaughter and gut the beasts before they even got here. Started to make them ice-cold an' all. That's progress for yer. It's lucky they decided to keep the older chaps on. At least you younger ones have a better chance of finding another job.

JIM. What chance have I got, Harry? I don't know no other work.

HARRY. There's no shortage of butcher's shops round here boy. Go and ask 'em if they're looking for a delivery boy.

JIM. But that wouldn't pay half of what I was getting. Besides, I don't know how to ride a bicycle.

HARRY. Oh, blimey, don't look now but there's Ellen the ever red. I'd best get back in ter work. Good luck, son.

(HE goes. ELLEN comes up to Jim.)

ELLEN. Harry? *(HE doesn't look at her.)* You got the push and all, Jim?

JIM. Yeah. Do you know where Kate is?

ELLEN. They've all gone running up to Creek Road to put themselves at Lady Helena's mercy.

JIM. Oh, maybe she'll be able to do something for me.

ELLEN. She'd have her work cut out then, wouldn't she—Trying to turn you into the shining ideal of christian womanhood.

JIM. Eh?

ELLEN. She ain't offering a service for men because she don't care how they carry on. It's women's behaviour she wants to change.

(Fade to POLLY and ANNIE.)

POLLY. Here Annie, what's it like? I mean how many days d'you get off? When do they pay yer? Do they give yer enough money to get home on yer day off?

ANNIE. Depends. They set the rules. Might get one Sunday afternoon off a month. I dunno. Seeing as it's the Cuttle-Smythes yer might get more.

POLLY. Do you get yer own room or do you have ter share?

ANNIE. Depends. You'll have to see when you gets there.

POLLY. S'pose they ask me to do something I've never heard of? What will I say?

ANNIE. You've heard of peeling potatoes, polishing floors, cleaning steps, washing curtains, washing pots, making tea, making a fire. They ain't going to ask you to fly in the air.

POLLY. No, I s'pose it's just common sense at the end of the day.

ANNIE. It's all the things yer hate doing when they're for yerself. Only you're going to have to do them for other people with a smile on yer chops.

POLLY. Yeah. I ain't looking forward to it.

(Fade to ELLEN and ANNIE.)

ELLEN. What'd she say?

ANNIE. She's fixed me up in service.

ELLEN. Annie what the hell are you doing? You know what it's like. I mean to the others it might be some sort of novelty but, Christ, surely you don't want to go back to that sorta life? Bowing and scraping and …

ANNIE. Ellen shut it will yer. I feel nervous enough. Don't make it worse. They can't all be the same, can they?

ELLEN. But …

ANNIE. I can't fall foul of Lady Helena now can I? I mean how can I say ter her "thank you very much but no thank you very much"? 'Cos there ain't no other work, and by the time I finds that out I can't then go on me hands and knees back to her 'cos by then she'll have plenty more deserving cases than me to place.

ELLEN. It's worth a try, honest it is.

ANNIE. You forget Ellen I've been on the streets once before. And, I can tell you, anything, yeah virtually anything, is better than that. I'm going to give this a try 'cos at the end of the day mate, what choice have I?

(Fade to ELLEN and MAGGIE.)

ELLEN. Mag, what's happened to the others?

MAGGIE. I dunno, there was so many asking fer help we lost each other. Polly got fixed up, straight off, I know that much. She starts work in the Cuttle-Smythe household.

ELLEN. But that bastard don't know her from Eve.

MAGGIE. No, but his wife does.

ELLEN. What about you?

MAGGIE. I didn't get no help at all, and what's more I ain't going to get none in the future 'cos I stopped going to her flaming club. So, Ellen, it looks like I'll have to come with you and try the jam factory.

ELLEN. They wouldn't take me on. I've been to every factory round here. They all say the same, only taking on girls with a reference from Lady Helena. I'm going to try down Southwark. Maybe her influence won't have travelled that far. Coming ...

MAGGIE. It's me Mum. She needs me at home.

ELLEN. She wouldn't have yer at home if you were in service.

MAGGIE. No, but she'd have the satisfaction of thinking I'd made something of meself. I'd better get back and let her know what's happened.

(ELLEN goes.
Fade to KATE comes up to JIM.)

KATE. What you doing here?

JIM. They decided to kick out the youngest chaps an' all.

KATE. What you going to do?

JIM. Harry says I should try for a job in a butcher's. What about you, how did you get on with Lady Helena?

KATE. She's fixed me up to see this family tomorrow for the position of general maid.

JIM. So much for our idea of getting a shop.

KATE. Them's dreams, Jim. Children's dreams.

JIM. We're nothing we are. If we live or die tomorrow nobody would care. Suppose this household don't want yer tomorrow?

KATE. Any girl what won't find work through no fault of her own is to be given seven shillings a week.

JIM. She's going to give money away?

KATE. Yeah, I'll say this for her, she's really putting herself out.

(Fade to MAGGIE and her MUM.)

EADY. You're tell me that even that dozy doe Polly got herself into a household with one of them joined together names. And you ain't got nothing.

MAGGIE. Yes, that's the long and the short of it.

EADY. Go back and ask her again—Lady Helena.

MAGGIE. I won't, I got more bloody pride.

EADY. Pride? Pride? You think you're a man you do.

MAGGIE. I don't.

EADY. What you got against being in service? Most normal, decent girls would jump at the chance.

MAGGIE. I don't want to …

EADY. It's only 'til yer get wed.

MAGGIE. I don't want to get married.

EADY. What are you going ter do then?

MAGGIE. Oh, I don't know, maybe I'll follow wonderful Helena's example, live on me own, devoting my life to the good of others.

EADY. At least she's got the respectability of widowhood. I tell you one thing, you ain't going to stop under this roof unless yer earns yer keep.

MAGGIE. See you in hell.

EADY. Not fer much longer, girl. Not unless yer get off yer backside.

(Fade to ELLEN, ANNIE, KATE, POLLY.)

ELLEN. D'you need any hands? No, I ain't had any experience of factory work but I worked down the gutting sheds in Deptford. I ain't had a day off sick ever. I'm a hard worker, honest, you only got to show me what to do, I'll pick it up, I'm a fast learner. Please take me on. Give me a chance. *(Pause.)* Oh no, I wouldn't have nothing to do with Trade Unions.

ANNIE. *(At the front door.)* Good morning madam, my name's …

KATE. *(At the front door.)* Good morning madam, my name's …

POLLY. *(At the front door.)* Good morning, Mrs. Cuttle-Smythe. Err, I'm not really sure like, should I have used the back door …?

Scene 7

Lady Helena's drawing room. LADY HELENA and EDWIN sit sorting through papers.

EDWIN. The apprentice fund is growing fatter by the day, Helena. By my reckoning you'll be able to admit another ten girls to your school of Domestic Economy.

LADY HELENA. (*Not listening.*) Priscilla should have been here half an hour ago.

EDWIN. Oh, I doubt if you'll see her again.

LADY HELENA. Why ever not?

EDWIN. She's got her pick of servants what does she need you for?

LADY HELENA. She's not like that, we've become good friends.

EDWIN. But she's such a sickly creature.

LADY HELENA. She was, but over the last few weeks, well, she's really come out of herself.

EDWIN. Helena, you can be so naive about people.

LADY HELENA. In what way?

EDWIN. The Cuttle-Smythes are after status. If enthusing about your hobby horse was part of the game, then so be it.

LADY HELENA. I don't agree with you at all. She's probably been laid up. Less gossip and more work is required.

LADY HELENA. (*To Edwin.*) See, that'll be her. Come in.

(EMILY enters.)

EMILY. There's a lady ...

LADY HELENA. Show her in Emily, you know
there's no need for formalities with Mrs. Cuttle-Smythe.

EMILY. Madam, it's not Mrs. Cuttle-Smythe. It's a,
er, lady, woman, one of them girls from the club.

LADY HELENA. Here?

EDWIN. The audacity.

LADY HELENA. Show her in Emily, please.

(MAGGIE enters. HELENA stands to great her.)

MAGGIE. I'm sorry to trouble you Lady Helena, but
I've come to ask for your help.

LADY HELENA. I remember you. You used to come
to the club didn't you? And *(Trying to remember.)* it's
Maggie isn't it?

MAGGIE. Yes it is, madam. You see since the sheds
closed down, I haven't been able to get work.

EDWIN. Only those who attended the club regularly can
now avail themselves of help.

(MAGGIE jumps, recognising Edwin.)

LADY HELENA. Quite so. Otherwise it wouldn't be
fair on those who did attend and are still looking for work.
Can I ask why you stopped coming?

*(Pause, MAGGIE sees EDWIN stare at her. SHE looks
from him to Helena and back to him.)*

MAGGIE. Me brother weren't well, madam. Me
Mother 'ad ter work evenings and I had to look after him.

LADY HELENA. Well ... I don't know.

MAGGIE. Please madam, me mother can't afford ter keep me. I have ter earn my way. I'll do any ... any reasonable work.

LADY HELENA. I was going to suggest my apprenticeship fund where you work for nothing but the fund pays you a small allowance.

MAGGIE. Would yer?

EDWIN.(*Cuts in.*) She's far too old Helena, the scheme's for thirteen to fifteen-year-olds. It would make a nonsense of it.

LADY HELENA. (*Turns to look at Edwin then back at Maggie*) Yes, I suppose that's right. There doesn't really seem much I can do at the moment but I will bear you in mind.

(SHE pulls the bell cord for EMILY who enters promptly.)

LADY HELENA. Emily, please show this young lady out and take her address.

(EMILY and MAGGIE walk out.)

MAGGIE. (*To Emily.*) Don't trouble yerself I ain't got one, me mum threw me out.

LADY HELENA. (*To Edwin.*) You were a bit hard on her, Edwin. I didn't like to contradict you but ...

EDWIN. Oh Helena, she was a trouble maker, she'll have to learn. You can't be too soft on that sort.

(Fade to ELLEN alone.)

ELLEN. I pawned all my books today, but it doesn't matter. It wouldn't have mattered in the end what I'd said or done. It wouldn't have made a shred of difference what five hundred of us had done. We'd still have been out of work. They'd still have got their way—those people with their schemes and funds and clubs and allowances—all thought up out of fear—out of a fear that we, the ones who made their wealth might get out of hand. So we need to be tamed and trained to succumb to their values and orders. What's the point of kicking against it when all you damage is your foot. And I'm left trying to explain myself to, yes, even to Jasper and Sebastian who reply, "But Ellen, at least she found them all work." Yes, but in service— in service. I could tell by the look on their faces that they couldn't see anything wrong. Why should they? After all isn't that what we're here for? You service your husband and your children. What's wrong with servicing those deemed better than you—at least you get paid for it. I don't want to keep arguing and kicking against it. I don't want to stick out like a sore thumb and be seen as odd. Who am I to call the others fools, when I am the biggest laughing stock of the lot—actually believing that I had any say over what happened to me or anyone else. (*SHE tears the pawn ticket into pieces and throws it on the floor.*)

(*Fade to LADY HELENA and ARTHUR.*)

LADY HELENA. Please sit down, Arthur. I'm most terribly sorry—about the loss of income. Priscilla did explain that it wasn't my doing?

ARTHUR. Oh yes. And in fact when the word got out that you'd gone to plead personally with the Corporation for a reversal of their decision I was able to sell, not as handsomely as I'd have wished, but not at a loss, as I'd originally feared. So I am quite satisfied with the outcome. Thank you.

LADY HELENA. Well, now, that is a relief.

ARTHUR. I have come to see you on a more delicate matter. That of my wife's health.

LADY HELENA. Goodness me. What's happened?

ARTHUR. Nothing. But, and I must come straight to the point, it is not doing her any good at all, participating in the club, and I have come to ask, now you have so many other capable volunteers, if my wife might be excused her duties and allowed to recuperate fully at home.

LADY HELENA. It seemed, if anything, that her interest in the club was boosting her self esteem.

ARTHUR. Quite the opposite I fear.

LADY HELENA. Well, she does still seem a bit edgy. I'm saddened. But Priscilla's well-being is of the utmost concern.

ARTHUR. Thank you for being so understanding.

LADY HELENA. Promise me one thing Arthur.

ARTHUR. Yes?

LADY HELENA. That you both won't desert me socially.

ARTHUR. I will promise you that with pleasure, Helena.

LADY HELENA. Good. You will be top of the invitation list for the forthcoming fête.

Scene 8

Priscilla's drawing room.

POLLY. They got a beautiful looking-glass in this room. As a special treat, I bring me old hat down here, only when I'm sure he's out and she's still a kip like, and I put it on and pretend all the girls are coming round for tea. (*SHE puts her hat on and straightens it. Whirls round to face the door. Putting on an upper class voice.*) Ellen, Maggie, Kate, Annie, lovies. So pleased you could come. Isn't this just splendid?

(*PRISCILLA walks in, POLLY stops. PRISCILLA stares at her.*)

POLLY. Sorry, madam.
PRISCILLA. Are you all right Polly?
POLLY. Yes, thank you, madam.
PRISCILLA. Did you buy that hat for your mother?
POLLY. Yes, madam, sorry, madam.
PRISCILLA. How is she?
POLLY. Very good, madam.
PRISCILLA. Oh? Cook told me, that she wasn't well?
POLLY. No, madam.
PRISCILLA. Why did you say "very good" then?
POLLY. Beggin' your pardon, madam.
PRISCILLA. Polly? Are you also trying to convince me that I'm mad?
POLLY. (*Blurts out.*) I'm sorry, madam, I am really but you know we only had time to learn how to say, "Yes, madam," "No, madam," "Begging your pardon," and "Very

good, madam." I'm afraid if I start talking normally you'll get offended.

PRISCILLA. Of course, that's good and proper in front of the master but you don't have to worry when it's just you and me. What were you doing just now?

POLLY. Trying me old hat on—to cheer meself up a bit like—(*Offering the hat.*) D'you wanna go?

PRISCILLA. (*Shakes her head but smiles.*) There is a quote, … a proverb, oh, I can't think …

POLLY. (*Tentatively.*) Blessed are the pure in hat?

PRISCILLA. No, it's not in the Bible. "Don't tame the wild God" that's it.

POLLY. Never heard that one. Are you all right, madam?

PRISCILLA. I'm sorry. It's a pagan sentiment—it means don't squash the spirit out of someone. Christianity can be a rather stifling ideology, don't you think?

POLLY. If you say so, madam.

(*ARTHUR comes in. THEY both freeze.*)

ARTHUR. Haven't you finished this room yet, girl?

PRISCILLA. Polly has scrubbed the kitchen from top to bottom. I have been supervising her.

ARTHUR. You got up at the appropriate time then? That's much better. I am pleased. (*To Polly.*) What on earth is that, girl? (*Meaning the hat.*)

PRISCILLA. We found it on the top shelf of the larder. The previous cook must have left it—if you remember she disappeared very abruptly.

ARTHUR. (*To Polly.*) Get rid of it.

PRISCILLA. Polly, please take that hat and dispose of it as you will.

POLLY. Yes, madam.

ARTHUR. *(To Priscilla.)* I'm pleased to see that you are learning to assert your authority with the servants at last.

Scene 9

LADY HELENA and EMILY.

LADY HELENA. Emily, would you mind putting my hair back up. It seems to be all awry.

EMILY. Very good, madam. *(EMILY stands behind Helena and does her hair.)*

LADY HELENA. Do you believe God answers prayer, Emily?

EMILY. Of course I do, madam.

LADY HELENA. When they are for ourselves only, of course. He is a little slow on the uptake. Rightly so, because selfishness should never be rewarded.

EMILY. No, madam.

LADY HELENA. But my prayers for those girls have been answered. As a species, they have been totally transformed. That is my reward. Do you remember the day I visited those sheds. You were very cynical about what could be achieved.

EMILY. Me? Why madam I'd never dream of being so presumptuous.

(Fade to the Pub. MAGGIE behind the bar. Sees ELLEN walk past in the street.)

MAGGIE. *(Calls out.)* Ellen, Ellen.

ELLEN. *(Puts her head round the door, then sees Maggie.)* Maggie, what you doing in here?

MAGGIE. It's good ter see yer. I thought you'd have been in before now.

ELLEN. Times have changed ain't they? Lady can't go fer a drink on her own these days.

MAGGIE. I called at your place but seems you moved.

ELLEN. Had to didn't I? Toff bought up all the places round Watergate Street, done 'em up with rents to match. I had to take lodgings with a family.

MAGGIE. Are you working?

ELLEN. I'm going for a job down the new button factory in Rotherhithe.

MAGGIE. *(Teasing.)* Got a union has it?

ELLEN. I don't know, do I. Fancy you working here. Still living at home are yer?

MAGGIE. Na, me mum threw me out.

ELLEN. So where yer living?

MAGGIE. Here.

ELLEN. Here? What happened to Len, then?

MAGGIE. I married him.

(ELLEN looks stunned.)

MAGGIE. Don't look like that, Ellen. *(Then.)* He don't trouble me often.

ELLEN. *(Aghast.)* You married Len?

MAGGIE. (*Angry.*) What bleedin' choices did I have, Ellen?

ELLEN. But what did you marry that great clod for?

(*LEN comes in.*)

LEN. Hello, Ellen, how are you?

ELLEN. (*Nicely embarrassed.*) Oh, hello Len, we was just talking about … the weather.

LEN. Chilly out, ain't it. (*To Maggie.*) Can you give us a hand in the yard, sweetheart? (*Kisses her on the cheek and goes.*)

MAGGIE. Be with you in a moment, dear. (*Wiping her cheek with her hand.*)

ELLEN. Sorry.

MAGGIE. What for, ain't your fault.

(*Fade to KATE and JIM, KATE is scrubbing the steps.*)

KATE. What are you doing here?

JIM. I thought I'd call by on my round and say hello.

KATE. Do you want to get me into trouble?

JIM. (*Grins.*) Chance would be a fine thing.

KATE. Don't you dare talk to me like that.

JIM. Sorry.

KATE. Can't you read? What does that notice say? There, in letters three inches high: "NO GENTLEMEN CALLERS."

JIM. But, I ain't a gentleman, I'm a bleedin' butcher's boy.

KATE. Jim, there is absolutely no need to swear. (*Pause.*) Listen, I'll try and slip out and meet yer tonight.

JIM. You said that last week, but you never turned up.

KATE. I can't help it if they've got eyes in their nightcaps. I'll try the best I can—now please go away.

Scene 10

Arthur and Priscilla's drawing room.

ARTHUR. My dear, all I am asking of you is that you make the effort and accompany me to the fête. It is not as if we are invited as guests of honour every day of the week, now is it?

PRISCILLA. (*Timidly.*) Please, you go dear. I don't feel well enough.

ARTHUR. You are my wife. It's your duty to come with me. Besides I promised Helena you'd be there. Stop this reclining nonsense. I thought that wretched club had knocked that sort of malingering out of you once and for all. Come and get your outdoor things on before it recurs.

PRISCILLA. She's bound to ask why you put a stop to me helping her.

ARTHUR. (*Patiently.*) I didn't put a stop to anything. We agreed, that you weren't suited to it. Besides she's far too well-mannered to bring the subject up.

PRISCILLA. She'll only feel obliged to ask how Polly's getting on. And I won't know how to explain that you want to get rid of her.

ARTHUR. You stupid woman, the girl's clumsy, incompetent and hopeless. Helena won't care a damn what I say about her and probably arrange to get us another.

Christ, servants are two a penny, they're nothing. Fancy worrying over a trifle like that. Your soft heart has contaminated your brain.

PRISCILLA. But she makes me laugh.

ARTHUR. All the more reason to come then—I never see you laugh.

PRISCILLA. Not Helena—Polly.

ARTHUR. (*Explodes.*) A servant is not supposed to make you laugh. They are to be seen and not heard, to know their place. How d'you expect to maintain any kind of discipline if you converse with them, as if they were part of your social circle?

PRISCILLA. Please, please, you go dear. I've plenty to be getting on with.

ARTHUR. (*Exasperated.*) The whole point of having servants in the first place is so women of your social standing don't have anything to get on with. (*More reasonable.*) My dear, if you carry on like this I shall be left without excuse or option but to call the doctor in, for there is plainly something wrong with your head.

PRISCILLA. It is not my head but my heart.

ARTHUR. Healthier looking women than you are filling up the asylums today.

PRISCILLA. (*Panics.*) No, I'm perfectly sane. Perfectly.

ARTHUR. Of course you're not, and I shall vouch for that fact, why would a sane woman refuse to see her friends?

PRISCILLA. They're not my friends, merely acquaintances of yours.

ARTHUR. Refuses to go out with her husband, refuses to leave the house, preferring instead the servants for entertainment. My dear, these are the values of a mad woman.

PRISCILLA. I am not mad, I am not mad, I am not mad.

ARTHUR. (*Very roughly, taking hold of her arm.*) You're ranting, you're raving.

PRISCILLA. Leave me be, leave me be.

ARTHUR. Now you, up. Come on. I'll get you outside the door if it kills me.

PRISCILLA. No, no, please, leave me alone.

(*POLLY enters carrying a full coal scuttle.*)

POLLY. Did you call me, sir?

PRISCILLA. Oh, Polly. (*SHE runs to her.*)

ARTHUR. No I didn't. Get out.

(*POLLY, shaken, as PRISCILLA almost knocks her over, drops the scuttle on the floor and the coal spills out over the carpet.*)

ARTHUR. (*Rounds on her.*) You stupid, clumsy, oaf.

POLLY. I am sorry, sir. (*SHE starts to pick up the pieces of coal.*)

ARTHUR. You are? You will be. Don't think you're taking this Sunday afternoon off or any other Sunday afternoon until you've made up the time to pay for it.

POLLY. Please. I will.

PRISCILLA. No, Arthur, her mother's not well, she must be allowed ...

ARTHUR. (*To Priscilla.*) Have you not a shred of loyalty to me?

(ARTHUR picks up the coal shovel. POLLY, having put all the coal back in the scuttle, stands.)

ARTHUR. I'll teach you a lesson you'll not forget.

PRISCILLA. No, no, please calm down dear, it was an accident.

POLLY. Er, no, look sir, say what you like, I'm sorry. But don't hit me.

ARTHUR. I can do what I like to you, I'm paying for you. Some men I know box their servants' ears for putting cutlery in the wrong drawer. Come here.

POLLY. (*Holds up her hands. Says placatingly.*) No-one has ever hit me sir. Not me mother, not me father, not me Guv'nor, not no one. I've taken a lot of abuse and no mistake but I won't be hit. (*Stronger.*) I'm warning you—I won 't be hit.

ARTHUR. We'll see about that.

(HE takes a swipe at her with the shovel. SHE brings her fist up and hits him with an almighty punch in the face. HE lands on the floor. PRISCILLA lets out a little cry. Her husband lies still. POLLY looks, then after a moment tentatively goes over to him, half expecting him to leap up at any minute.)

POLLY. Oh, my God, Oh, Jesus, Jesus Christ. I think I've done for him, miss.

PRISCILLA. Go to the kitchen Polly, get me some lard.

POLLY. Madam?

PRISCILLA. I'll grease his shoe and the floor.

POLLY. (*Swallows.*) Madam?
PRISCILLA. (*Shaking.*) It's worth a try.

(*ARTHUR, having only been knocked unconscious, lifts his arm to his head and groans. POLLY steps back in fright, PRISCILLA sits down.*)

PRISCILLA. Will you go and fetch the doctor, Polly.
POLLY. Me??
PRISCILLA . (*Gets up.*) No, I'll go ...
POLLY. I can't be here not when ... he comes to his senses.
PRISCILLA. No.

(*POLLY runs off.*)

Scene 11

ANNIE sits alone on Blackheath.

ANNIE. They has their tea early on Sunday—three o'clock. And then I'm allowed to do what I want, as long as I'm back for six-thirty. And I come up here for some fresh air and I gulps it down. I sit here on me own, and I think, "It's me. I'm here and I'm breathing."

(*Some distance away SHE sees Kate, pushing a pram.*)

ANNIE. (*Squinting.*) That looks like ... It is ... I don't believe it. (*SHE gets up, calls.*) Kate. (*Runs up to Kate, calling. KATE doesn't turn but continues to push the pram. Breathless, ANNIE catches up with her.)* Kate, it's me.

(KATE looks at her, then around, nervously.)

ANNIE. Kate. It's me Annie.

KATE. (*Hisses.*) I know. I should think every soul on Blackheath knows.

ANNIE. Well, how are you, ain't you pleased to see me? (*To the pram.*) Is it a boy or a girl?

KATE. I'm well thank you. This is Master John. I'm allowed to look after him on Nanny's day off.

ANNIE. (*Sarcastically.*) Ain't that nice for you.

KATE. (*Seriously.*) Yes, they say I've the potential to become a Nanny. (*SHE continues to look around her.*)

ANNIE. They would wouldn't they. 'Ere what d'you keep looking over yer shoulder for?

KATE. It won't do us any good if they see us talking together.

ANNIE. You what? What, they got a spy glass from their windows then, that can see round corners and through houses?

(KATE starts walking on. ANNIE has to catch up with her.)

ANNIE. What you walking away from me for? Kate, it's me. Annie.

KATE. Annie, look. It's no good hankering after what was. We've got to try and make the best of what we've got, and I, for one am trying to better myself. If you've got any sense you'll try and do the same. (*SHE turns.*)

ANNIE. (*Catches hold of Kate's arm.*) What you frightened of? That I'll snatch the son and heir and hold him to ransom?

KATE. That's just it—isn't it. Some of us are trying to forget who we are, where we come from and put the past behind us, but no, Polly goes and bangs her fist in her employer's face. And it's like we're all under suspicion.

ANNIE. You're telling me? Suspicion. You know what mine have taken to doing, eh? Only locking me in me room at night. They think I don't know but I hear the key go. Then they have to unlock it really early so I can get up and do all the chores before they get up proper. Bet if there was a fire they'd forget to unlock the bloody door at all.

KATE. Thanks to Polly.

ANNIE. Poor Polly.

KATE. She could have killed him.

ANNIE. I don't see that by talking to me you'll get into trouble. What's that got to do with anything.

KATE. She ain't been seen of since—they might think we've got something to do with her, or we're hiding her, or anything. We got to prove to them we aren't all like that.

ANNIE. Let me put your mind at rest Kate. They caught her, the police, she's in Holloway.

KATE. How do you know?

ANNIE. Oh, don't they allow you to read the papers then—this household where they're so keen for advancement of general maids to nannies?

KATE. Actually, I don't have to lay out the fires, they have another maid to do that. So I don't get to see the old newspapers. (*Pause.*) And, I'm sorry, but I really do have to go. (*SHE does so.*)

ANNIE. (*Shouts after her. Not caring who hears.*) You want to know how I get to read them? Because them what I works for are so bleedin' mean. They make me put newspaper all over the carpet so it don't wear, then when they know company's coming they make me take it all up. I gets to know all the news that way. Everything they got is for show. They're so tight, that when they walk their arses squeak.

(Fade to MAGGIE and PRISCILLA.)

MAGGIE. I know what she done like weren't right.

PRISCILLA. Please, please could you sit down and keep your voice down. My husband's upstairs and the doctor says he's to stay in bed and have plenty of rest.

MAGGIE. I'm sorry about that, I mean I know how you must feel. (*Gulps down the insincerity.*) I have got a husband of me own like. But, me and Polly worked together fer years. She weren't the sort to start a fight or nothing—even if there was an argument she'd be the one to smooth things over.

(PRISCILLA doesn't respond.)

MAGGIE. Couldn't you like give her a good character? I mean I could, but it don't mean nothing coming from me.

PRISCILLA. I can't give evidence against my husband in a Court of Law.

MAGGIE. Well, can't you have a word with him? I mean I ain't suggesting you take Polly back, just drop the charges.

PRISCILLA. You don't understand ...

MAGGIE. I know it ain't on. To go round smacking people on the jaw. It ain't right, and I know it, but I'm sure she never meant to kill him. (*Pause.*) And let's face it, if it was the other way round and he'd'ave hit her, no one would even have heard about it.

PRISCILLA. It isn't that simple.

MAGGIE. (*Angry.*) Oh, but it is. To your sort everything is. Bet you had one of them real pretty dolls' houses when you was a little girl and you grew up to live in one of your own, except it's got real people in it not dolls. When you don't like one of 'em for whatever reason you just get rid of 'em, throw them away ...

PRISCILLA. That's not fair.

MAGGIE. No, it's not. You got a responsibility, Mrs. Cuttle-Smythe not only to yourself, but to Polly.

Scene 12

LEN and JIM in the pub.

LEN. D'you reckon they'll hang her then?

JIM. Dunno. He's claiming she intended to murder him.

LEN. You'd think he'd have more vanity than ter stand in the Old Bailey and admit that slip of a maid chinned and floored him.

JIM. A slip of a girl? Polly? It's your memory what's slipping.

LEN. Yeah, but she's still only a woman, when all's said and done. Unless you know something I don't.

JIM. But, you never know though what folks are capable of, do yer?

LEN. True. (*Pause.*) Hope your Kate ain't like that.

JIM. Na, different girl she is, being so close to her betters has changed her for the better I can tell you.

LEN. A lady.

JIM. Yes I s'pose she is. Treats me with courtesy and respect these days …

LEN. You lucky bleeder … Mag could do with that sort of training I can tell yer …

JIM. Where is she?

LEN. You may well ask … said she needed some fresh air … said she weren't feeling too good … If you ask me I think it was too much helping herself to the profits last night. Here, (*HE beckons Jim closer.*) she err, your Kate, did she ever bring anything up in conversation about um, sausage skins?

JIM. Take no notice, Len. I never. I told her straight and she ain't likely to bring it up again … she's too well spoken these days to refer to sausages in any conversation except one concerning breakfast.

LEN. I don't know where they all think it up from, do you?

JIM. Don't bear thinking about does it.

(*Pause.*)

LEN. We could take a tip off them toffs, Jim and no mistake. Look at what our women get away with, eh?

JIM. How d'you mean?

LEN. When we're boys we have to bring our wages straight home to our mothers, right? And she gives us pocket money out of it. And what happens when we're men? We give our wages to our wives and they give us our beer money. Now, you don't get that sorta behaviour from ladies do yer? It's all "please could I have some housekeeping money, my darling." See we've got it wrong all these years, boy.

JIM. You got a point there Len, and no mistake.

LEN. Still, I can't stand round here discussing how to change the world all day. What you got for me this week, Jim?

JIM. Sorry, I was forgetting ... (*Taking out a package and giving it to Len.*)

LEN. (*Looking inside.*) Bleedin' hell. Sausages! What you trying to do to me boy?

Scene 13

LADY HELENA sits, writing in her journal. ELLEN talks to the audience. ANNIE, KATE, MAGGIE and POLLY stand, separately alone.

LADY HELENA. This morning I woke up and I felt like hugging myself.

ELLEN. It's hardly what you'd call a rewarding job.

LADY HELENA. The careful planning and hard work has been of benefit to so many.

ELLEN. You put a button on a metal plate, then cover it with material.

ANNIE. This morning I woke up and I realised that I hadn't dreamed about running away for a whole week. It's much better not to hold on to your dreams. I suppose it's natural to let go of them as you get older.

LADY HELENA. It was of course a blow, when the girls were unexpectedly thrown out of work.

ELLEN. You bring the lever down.

LADY HELENA. But even that turned to our advantage, giving the coarsest girl a sense of urgency.

MAGGIE. I wanted something more for myself, but me mother was right. You got to make the best of what you got. It's easier to be ordinary, ter do what's expected of yer. It's just I wanted something more.

ELLEN. And there you have a perfectly covered button.

LADY HELENA. Through diligence and persistence even the rawest of material has been transformed into a servant of lower middle class acceptability.

KATE. I've been admired for looking nice and dressing nice, I feel really special when men catch my eye. No one would dream of calling me common now. I know what to expect of them and they know what to expect of me. If a man swore in front of me today, he'd be mortified. I've earned that sort of respect.

ELLEN. At the end of the day you have a whole box full.

LADY HELENA. Two hundred and fifty of them placed to date in good households.

ELLEN. The conditions are cleaner but the whole place is very hot and noisy.

LADY HELENA. One tale of woe, Polly, an aberration.

POLLY. It struck me this morning that I've always been at someone's mercy ... We all are when we're born an' that. It's after that, things unequal out a bit. I was at the mercy of the guv'nors in the sheds. I was at the mercy of the master in the house. And now I'm at the mercy of the law.

ELLEN. It makes it impossible to talk.

LADY HELENA. And one regret, namely Priscilla, who I've not seen since the incident.

ELLEN. The only variety in the work is when they change the quality of the material.

LADY HELENA. But I cannot help but marvel, modesty permitting, at the accomplishment.

ELLEN. But they have a works canteen here, thanks to the union.

LADY HELENA. Even the doubting Thomases have had to eat their words.

ELLEN. (*Referring to a woman she works with, not Polly.*) See that woman—over there? She started it; she even gives speeches in public—you'd never think it would yer—People think she's mad.

LADY HELENA. (*Turns.*) Priscilla, whan an unexpected surprise. (*SHE gets up and goes.*)

ELLEN. But she ain't ... She says to me, "Ellen, we got a right, and a responsibility to speak out." I looked at her just like Maggie used to look at me an' I says, "Good job we're only here once." "So," she says, "you just going to sit there and let it happen again, then?"

End of Play

NOTES ON THE FIRST PRODUCTION

The Gut Girls was commissioned by Teddy Kiendl, who was the Artistic Director of the Albany Empire Theatre in Deptford. He decided, wisely, that no real meat should be used in the production. However, it is a compliment to the Designer, Kate Owen, and production team that the critic from the Independent Newspaper put in her review; "You need a strong stomach for this show, to steel yourself against the stinking innards and swilling blood." It is, therefore, crucial to make the meat as realistic as possible.

The Albany is built in the round and the play was written with this in mind.

The main playing area was a large wooden floor, and in the first scene there were two butchers' tables where the girls worked. Splitting the focus like this seemed to aid the dialogue.

The set had six carcasses (not real) hanging above it. There were no blackouts between the scenes, and props and furniture were kept to a minimum. For example, a small carpet and a Victorian upright chair were used to create Lady Helena's drawing room. The smaller scenes were set around the circumference of the main playing area and lit selectively; so for example, scene four was created by Edna (Polly's Mother) sitting on a low stool peeling potatoes, the mangle used in scene seven was left on set throughout the first half, and Ellen's room (scene five) was created by putting a rag rug on the floor.

The main consideration for the Designer when creating the costumes was the amount of doubling of parts. The girls, for example, wore petticoats underneath their Gut Girl clothes, which then became their maids' costumes.

The gutting sheds were very cold, and although there is a line in the play about the girls having to wear two coats, this becomes very uncomfortable for actors on stage under lights. For this production, they wore men's jackets over leg o'mutton blouses, sacking aprons, woollen skirts, fingerless mittens and clogs.

It is obvious from the text that the girls wore colourful clothes and, when out, picture hats, whilst Lady Helena et al wear clothes which, although more grand, are very sober in colour and style.

Of course, it won't always be possible to perform the play in the round, but it is important to try and have the scenes flowing into one another as smoothly as possible, to maintain the energy of the piece.

TWO NEW COMEDIES FROM
━━━━━ SAMUEL FRENCH, Inc.━━━━━

FAST GIRLS. **(Little Theatre). Comedy.** Diana Amsterdam. 2m., 3f. Int. Lucy Lewis is a contemporary, single woman in her thirties with what used to be called a "healthy sex life," much to the chagrin of her mother, who feels Lucy is too fast, too easy—and too single. Her best friend, on the other hand, neighbor Abigail McBride, is deeply envious of Lucy's ease with men. When Lucy wants to date a man she just calls him up, whereas Abigail sits home alone waiting for Ernest, who may not even know she exists, to call. The only time Abigail isn't by the phone is after Lucy has had a hot date, when she comes over to Lucy's apartment to hear the juicy details and get green with envy. Sometimes, though, Lucy doesn't want to talk about it, which drives Abigail *nuts* ("If you don't tell me about men I have no love life!"). Lucy's mother arrives to take the bull by the horns, so to speak, arriving with a challenge. Mom claims no man will marry Lucy (even were she to *want to* get married), because she's too easy. Lucy takes up the challenge, announcing that she is going to get stalwart ex-boyfriend Sidney ("we're just friends") Epstein to propose to her. Easier said than done. Sidney doesn't *want* a fast girl. Maybe dear old Mom is right, thinks Lucy. Maybe fast girls *can't* have it all. "Amsterdam makes us laugh, listen and think."—Daily Record. "Brilliantly comic moments."—The Monitor. "rapidly paced comedy with a load of laughs . . . a funny entertainment with some pause for reflection on today's [sexual] confusion."—Suburban News. "Takes a penetrating look at [contemporary sexual chaos]. Passion, celibacy, marriage, fidelity are just some of the subjects that Diana Amsterdam hilariously examines."—Tribune News. **(#8149)**

ADVICE FROM A CATERPILLAR. **(Little Theatre.) Comedy.** Douglas Carter Beane. 2m. 2f. 1 Unit set & 1 Int. Ally Sheedy and Dennis Christopher starred in the delightful off-Broadway production of this hip new comedy. Ms. Sheedy played Missy, an avant garde video artist who specializes in re-runs of her family's home videos, adding her own disparaging remarks. Needless to say, she is very alienated from the middle-class, family values she grew up with, which makes her very *au courant*, but strangely unhappy. She has a successful career and a satisfactory love-life with a businessman named Suit. Suit's married, but that doesn't stop him and Missy from carrying on. Something's missing, though—and Missy isn't sure what it is, until she meets Brat. He is a handsome young aspiring actor. Unfortunately, Brat is also the boyfriend of Missy's best friend. Sound familiar? It isn't—because Missy's best friend is a gay man named Spaz! Spaz has been urging Missy to find an unmarried boyfriend, but this is too much—too much for Spaz, too much for Suit and, possibly, too much for Missy. Does she *want* a serious relationship (ugh—how bourgeois!)? Can a bisexual unemployed actor actually be her Mr. Wonderful? "Very funny ... a delightful evening."—Town & Village. **(#3876)**

I STAND BEFORE YOU NAKED

by Joyce Carol Oates
Monologues

(Little Theatre) 11f. (doubling possible—original production was done with 6f.) Bare stage. This extraordinary new collection of dramatic monologues by one of America's foremost novelists, poets, essayists and women of letters rivals *Talking With* in dramatic intensity, language and sheer weirdness. The evening begins and ends with the title poem, a haunting evocation of Woman on the edge of the madness of vulnerability. There is humor here, but mostly the monologues grip us in the firm hold of a master writer interested more in the pathetic, the strange, the horrifying. In other words, this is vintage Joyce Carol Oates. Contains the following monologues: "Little Blood Button," "Wife of," "Wealthy Lady," "The Boy," "The Orange," "Good Morning, Good Afternoon," "Darling, I'm Telling You (Angel Eyes)," "Nuclear Holocaust," "Slow Motion," "Pregnant."   (#11681)

VITAL SIGNS

by Jane Martin
Monologue play

(Little Theatre) 2m., (optional), 6f. Bare stage. The mysterious, pseudonymous Louisvillian, author of the acclaimed *Talking With,* has never been funnier, or more dramatically compelling, than in this extraordinary suite of theatrical miniatures, over thirty monologues with a length of around two minutes each, for six actresses. The two men in the play are "foils" for these compelling women. Although they do speak in one piece, their presence in your cast may be optional. Somehow, all the pieces add up to a collage of contemporary woman in all her warmth and majesty, her fear and frustration, her joy and her sadness. *Vital Signs* wowed them at the Humana Festival at Actors Theatre of Louisville, where its exciting first production was staged by Artistic Director Jon Jory. Included in our book are the details of Mr. Jory's direction which kept the theatrical ball rolling, headed into the pocket for a strike. "It does not just celebrate language from colorful women; [it] does the hoe-down."—Detroit Free Press. The New York Times praised "the continuing vitality and originality of the author's voice." "Offers wonderful opportunities for actresses to show off their versatility."—Washington Times. "Martin's eye and ear for the texture of everyday life in this culture is as playfully accurate as Lily Tomlin and Jane Wagner's. She's a fine quipster; but she manages, too, to open little windows of sadness into women's souls."—Detroit News.   (#24019)

Other Publications For Your Interest

RAVENSCROFT. (Little Theatre.) Mystery. Don Nigro. 1m., 5f. Simple unit set. This unusual play is several cuts above the genre it explores, a Gothic thriller for groups that don't usually do such things, a thinking person's mystery, a dark comedy that is at times immensely funny and at others quite frightening. On a snowy night, Inspector Ruffing is called to a remote English country house to investigate the headlong plunge of a young manservant, Patrick Roarke, down the main staircase, and finds himself getting increasingly involved in the lives of five alluring and dangerous women— Marcy, the beautiful Viennese governess with a past, Mrs. Ravenscroft, the flirtatious and chattery lady of the manor, Gillian, her charming but possibly demented daughter, Mrs. French, the formidable and passionate cook, and Dolly, a frantic and terrified little maid—who lead him through an increasingly bewildering labyrinth of contradictory versions of what happened to Patrick and to the dead Mr. Ravenscroft before him. There are ghosts at the top of the staircase, skeletons in the closet, and much more than the Inspector had bargained for as his quest to solve one mystery leads him deeper and deeper into others and to an investigation of his own tortured soul and the nature of truth itself. You will not guess the ending, but you will be teased, seduced, bewildered, amused, frightened and led along with the Inspector to a dark encounter with truth, or something even stranger. A funny, first rate psychological mystery, and more.

(#19987)

DARK SONNETS OF THE LADY, THE. (Advanced Groups.) Drama. Don Nigro. 4m., 4f. Unit set. First produced professionally at the McCarter Theatre in Princeton and a finalist for the National Play Award, this stunningly theatrical and very funny drama takes place in Vienna in the fall of the year 1900, when Dora, a beautiful and brilliant young girl, walks into the office of Sigmund Freud, then an obscure doctor in his forties, to begin the most famous and controversial encounter in the history of psychoanalysis. Dora is funny, suspicious, sarcastic and elusive, and Freud become fascinated and obsessed by her and by the intricate labyrinth of her illness. He moves like a detective through the mystery of her life, and we meet in the course of his journey through her mind: her lecherous father, her obsessively house-cleaning mother, her irritating brother, her sinister admirer Herr Klippstein and his sensual and seductive wife, and their pretty and lost little governess. Nightmares, fantasies, hallucinations and memories all come alive onstage in a wild kaleidoscopic tapestry as Freud moves closer and closer to the truth about Dora's murky past, and the play becomes a kind of war between the two of them about what the truth is, about the uneasy truce between men and women, and ultimately a tragic love story. Laced throughout with eerie and haunting Strauss waltzes, this is a rich, complex, challenging and delightfully intriguing universe, a series of riddles one inside the other that lead the audience step by step to the center of Dora's troubled soul and her innermost secrets. Is Dora sick, or is the corrupt patriarchal society in which she and Freud are both trapped the real source of a complex group neurosis that binds all the characters together in a dark web of desperate erotic relationships, a kind of beautiful, insane and terrible dance of life, desire and death?

(#5952)

CEMENTVILLE
by Jane Martin
Comedy
Little Theatre

(5m., 9f.) Int. The comic sensation of the 1991 Humana Festival at the famed Actors Theatre of Louisville, this wildly funny new play by the mysterious author of *Talking With* and *Vital Signs* is a brilliant portrayal of America's fascination with fantasy entertainment, "the growth industry of the 90's." We are in a run-down locker room in a seedy sports arena in the Armpit of the Universe, "Cementville, Tennessee," with the scurviest bunch of professional wrasslers you ever saw. This is decidedly a small-time operation—not the big time you see on TV. The promoter, Bigman, also appears in the show. He and his brother Eddie are the only men, though; for the main attraction(s) are the "ladies." There's Tiger, who comes with a big drinking problem and a small dog; Dani, who comes with a large chip on her shoulder against Bigman, who owes all the girls several weeks' pay; Lessa, an ex-Olympic shotputter with delusions that she is actually employed presently in athletics; and Netty, an overweight older woman who appears in the ring dressed in baggy pajamas, with her hair in curlers, as the character "Pajama Mama." There is the eager-beaver go-fer Nola, a teenager who dreams of someday entering the glamorous world of pro wrestling herself. And then, there are the Knockout Sisters, refugees from the Big Time but banned from it for heavy-duty abuse of pharmaceuticals as well as having gotten arrested *in flagrante delicto* with the Mayor of Los Angeles. They have just gotten out of the slammer; but their indefatigable manager, Mother Crocker ("Of the Auto-Repair Crockers") hopes to get them reinstated, if she can keep them off the white powder. Bigman has hired the Knockout Sisters as tonight's main attraction, and the fur really flies along with the sparks when the other women find out about the Knockout Sisters. Bigman has really got his hands full tonight. He's gotta get the girls to tear each other up in the ring, not the locker room; he's gotta deal with tough-as-nails Mother Crocker; he's gotta keep an arena full of tanked-up rubes from tearing up the joint—and he's gotta solve the mystery of who bit off his brother Eddie's dick last night.   (#5580)

THE BABY DANCE
Little Theatre-Drama
by Jane Anderson

3m., 2f. 2 Ints. Stephanie Zimbalist starred in the original production of this brilliant, moving new drama, both at the Pasadena Playhouse and at the Long Wharf Theatre. She played a woman from Los Angeles named Rachel who has everything she wants in life—except a child. Rachel has located a poor couple who have more children than they can afford to keep, and have agreed to let their latest, when it is born, be adopted by Rachel and her husband. Desperate for a healthy baby, Rachel is paying for all of the poor woman's pre-natal care and hospital expenses. When she arrives for a visit at the trailer park where Al and Wanda live, she is appalled to find that Wanda is not eating correctly. She is also appalled by Al, who actually comes on to her when he is not seething with resentment. The whole arrangement nearly falls through, but by the second act, both couples are back on track. Until, that is, it is learned that the newborn baby may—just may—have suffered some brain damage in the difficult birth, causing Wanda's husband to back away from the deal, much to Rachel's chagrin. Rachel wants the baby anyway, wants to take the chance. In the end, the childless couple do renege on the deal, leaving Wanda and Al with yet another mouth to feed. "The best play produced this season at the Long Wharf Theatre and the first in several seasons to touch the heart so profoundly."—New Haven Advocate. *The Baby Dance* is not just a 'woman's play.' It is a gripping drama that leaves the audience with more empathy for these people than they would have thought possible."—Bridgeport Post. "A powerful, deeply wrenching drama."—Berkshire Eagle. "It would take a heart of stone to be unmoved by Jane Anderson's *The Baby Dance*.".   (#4305)

THE BATTLE OF SHALLOWFORD
Little Theatre-Comedy
by Ed Simpson

8m., 1f. Int. On a quiet Sunday night, the local regulars have gathered at Burton Mock's general store, in the small town of Shallowford, NC. It is October, 1938. The rest of the world is poised on the brink of war, but the locals aren't much worried about events in the world at large. They're more interested in the local gossip—and Burton's general store is the best place to hear it. The regulars include the gossipy, whining Clunette; fey church choirmaster Fred; lowlife, wild-eyed Newsome Jarvis, on hand with his "slow" son, Doodad; Mr. Roy, a one-armed World War I veteran who holds court at the store; egotistic local football hero Dewey Sowers; Burton's restless young daughter, Ruthie; and her schoolmate Lonny Hutchins, a sci-fi aficionado. All is calm; until, that is, they turn on the radio and learn that the Martians have invaded! Of course, it is the famous Orson Welles broadcast they are listening to—but they fall for it hook, line and shotgun, and run out to do battle against the fearsome threat from the invading Martians. Only Lonny suspects that something is fishy, but he's got his hands full if he thinks he's gonna deter the local yokels from their moment of glory. This delightful new comedy has had several successful productions nation-wide, and is finally available to y'all. Read it if you want a good laugh; produce it if that's how you like your audience to respond. "A theatrical gem."—Asheville Citizen-Times. "Tickle their funny bones, warm their hearts, don't insult their intelligence ... Ed Simpson's *The Battle of Shallowford* hits that magic trio."—Knoxville News-Sentinel. "A sentimental comedy that's hilariously on target. It could easily become a community theatre staple in much the way the works of Larry Shue have."—Knoxville Journal. A cassette tape of excerpts from the Mercury Theatre's radio broadcast of "The War of the Worlds" called for in the text of the play is available for $10, plus postage.   (#4315)